Grand Cote
National Wildlife Refuge

Comprehensive Conservation Plan

Northern Pintail

Photo Credit to: Dave Menke
USFWS Photo

Comprehensive Conservation Plans provide long-term guidance for management decisions; set forth goals, objectives, and strategies needed to accomplish refuge purposes; and identify the Fish and Wildlife Service's best estimate of future needs. These plans detail program planning levels that are sometimes substantially above current budget allocations and, as such, are primarily for Service strategic planning and program prioritization purposes. The plans do not constitute a commitment for staffing increases, operational and maintenance increases, or funding for future land acquisition.

Grand Cote National Wildlife Refuge

Comprehensive Conservation Plan

U.S. Department of the Interior
Fish and Wildlife Service
Southeast Region

November 2006

Submitted by: _____ Date: **8-10-06**
Andrew Hammond, Refuge Manager
Grand Cote NWR

Concur: _____ Date: **9/21/06**
Louis Hinds, Refuge Supervisor
Southeast Region

Concur: _____ Date: **9-28-06**
Jon Andrew, Regional Chief
Southeast Region

Approved by: _____ Date: **9/25/06**
Acting Sam Hamilton, Regional Director
Southeast Region

COMPREHENSIVE CONSERVATION PLAN

GRAND COTE NATIONAL WILDLIFE REFUGE
Avoyelles Parish, Louisiana

U.S. Department of the Interior
Fish and Wildlife Service
Southeast Region
Atlanta, Georgia

November 2006

TABLE OF CONTENTS

SECTION A. COMPREHENSIVE CONSERVATION PLAN

I. BACKGROUND 1

    Introduction...1
    Purpose and Need for the Plan 1
    Fish and Wildlife Service 1
    National Wildlife Refuge System 2
    Legal Policy Context...3
    National and International Conservation Plans and Initiatives 3
        North American Bird Conservation Initiative 4
        North American Waterfowl Management Plan 4
        Partners in Flight Bird Conservation Plan 4
        U.S. Shorebird Conservation Plan 4
        North American Waterbird Conservation Plan 4
        U.S. Woodcock Plan 5
    Relationship To State Wildlife Agency..5

II. REFUGE OVERVIEW...7

    Introduction...7
    Refuge History and Purpose 7
    Special Designations 10
        Wilderness Review...10
    Ecosystem Context..10
    Regional Conservation Plans and Initiatives 11
    Regional Conservation Plans and Initiatives 12
        Lower Mississippi River Ecosystem Plan...12
        North American Waterfowl Management Plan 12
        PartnerS in Flight 12
        U.S. Shorebird Conservation Plan 13
        U.S. Shorebird Conservation Plan 13
        North American Bird Conservation Initiative 13
        U.S. Woodcock Plan 13
    Ecological Threats and Problems...13
        Forest Loss and Fragmentation 13
        Alterations to Hydrology 15
        Siltation of Aquatic Ecosystems 16
        Proliferation of Invasive Aquatic Plants 16
    Physical Resources 16
        Climate...16
        Geology and Topography..17
        Soils 18
        Hydrology 18
        Water Quality and Quantity 19
    Biological Resources 20
        Habitat..20
        Wildlife...26
    Cultural Resources 30
    Socioeconomic Environment 31

Early Settlement of Avoyelles Parish 31
Land Use 32
Demographics 32
Employment 32
Recreation 32
Transportation 33
Visitor Services 33
Hunting 34
Fishing 34
Non-consumptive Uses 34
Refuge Administration 36

III. PLAN DEVELOPMENT 37
Public Involvement and the Planning Process 37
Summary of Issues, Concerns, and Opportunities 37
Fish and Wildlife Population Management 38
Habitat Management 39
Resource Protection 40
Visitor Services 40
Refuge Administration 41

IV. MANAGEMENT DIRECTION 43
Introduction 43
Vision 44
Goals, Objectives, and Strategies 44
Fish and Wildlife Population Management 45
Habitat Management 54
Resource Protection 57
Visitor Services 60
Refuge Administration 66

V. PLAN IMPLEMENTATION 69
Introduction 69
Projects 69
Fish And Wildlife Population Management 70
Habitat Management 71
Resource Protection 73
Visitor Services 74
Refuge Administration 75
Funding and Personnel 75
Volunteers/Partnership Opportunities 76
Step-Down Management Plans 76
Monitoring and Adaptive Management 78
Plan Review and Revision 79

SECTION B. APPENDICES

APPENDIX I. GLOSSARY 81

APPENDIX II. REFERENCES AND LITERATURE CITED 89

APPENDIX III. RELEVANT LEGAL MANDATES 95

APPENDIX IV. PUBLIC INVOLVEMENT...103
    Public Involvement Process 103
    Draft Plan Comments and Service Response...103

APPENDIX V. COMPATIBILITY DETERMINATION 107

APPENDIX VI. INTRA-SERVICE SECTION 7 BIOLOGICAL EVALUATION 121

APPENDIX VII. REFUGE BIOTA..125

APPENDIX VIII. LIST OF PREPARERS..135

APPENDIX IX. BUDGET REQUESTS...137

APPENDIX X. FINDING OF NO SIGNIFICANT IMPACT..139

LIST OF FIGURES

Figure 1.   The Location of Central Louisiana National Wildlife Refuge Complex in Avoyelles Parish, Louisiana. 8
Figure 2.   Current and Approved Acquisition Boundary of Grand Cote National Wildlife Refuge. 9
Figure 3.   Mississippi Alluvial Valley. 11
Figure 4.   Forest Cover Changes in the Mississippi Alluvial Valley...14
Figure 5.   General Habitat Types on Grand Cote National Wildlife Refuge. 22
Figure 6.   Waterfowl Impoundments in the West Farm Unit, Grand Cote National Wildlife Refuge...23
Figure 7.   Waterfowl Impoundments in the East Farm Unit, Grand Cote National Wildlife Refuge....24
Figure 8.   Current visitor facilities on Grand Cote National Wildlife Refuge. 35
Figure 9.   Proposed wildlife observation and photography and environmental education and interpretation visitor facilities on Grand Cote National Wildlife Refuge. 62
Figure 10. Current and proposed hunting and fishing visitor facilities on Grand Cote National Wildlife Refuge..63

LIST OF TABLES

Table 1.   Summary of existing habitat types at Grand Cote National Wildlife Refuge.......................21
Table 2.   Louisiana step-down and Mississippi Flyway objectives 38
Table 3.   Summary of Grand Cote National Wildlife Refuge Comprehensive Conservation Plan projects. 69
Table 4.   Grand Cote National Wildlife Refuge step-down management plans related to the goals and objectives portion of the Comprehensive Conservation Plan. 76

I. Background

INTRODUCTION

This Comprehensive Conservation Plan for Grand Cote National Wildlife Refuge was prepared to guide management actions and direction for the refuge. Fish and wildlife conservation will receive first priority in refuge management; wildlife-dependent recreation will be allowed and encouraged as long as it is compatible with, and does not detract from, the mission of the refuge or the purposes for which it was established.

A planning team developed a range of alternatives that best met the goals and objectives of the refuge and that could be implemented within the 15-year planning period. The draft comprehensive conservation plan and environmental assessment, prepared for this refuge, described the Fish and Wildlife Service's proposed plan, as well as other alternatives considered and their effects on the environment. The draft plan and environmental assessment was made available to state and federal government agencies, conservation partners, and the general public for review and comment. Comments from each entity were considered in the development of this final plan.

PURPOSE AND NEED FOR THE PLAN

The purpose of the plan is to develop an action that best achieves the refuge purpose; attains the vision and goals developed for the refuge; contributes to the National Wildlife Refuge System mission; addresses key problems, issues and relevant mandates; and is consistent with sound principles of fish and wildlife management.

Specifically, the plan is needed to:

- Provide a clear statement of refuge management direction;
- Provide refuge neighbors, visitors, and government officials with an understanding of Service management actions on and around the refuge;
- Ensure that Service management actions, including land protection and recreation/education programs, are consistent with the mandates of the National Wildlife Refuge System; and
- Provide a basis for the development of budget requests for operations, maintenance, and capital improvement needs.

One of the greatest needs of the Service is communication with the public and the public's participation in carrying out the mission of the National Wildlife Refuge System. Many agencies, organizations, institutions, and businesses have developed relationships with the Service to advance the mission of national wildlife refuges.

FISH AND WILDLIFE SERVICE

As part of its mission, the Service manages more than 540 national wildlife refuges covering over 95 million acres. These areas comprise the National Wildlife Refuge System, the world's largest collection of lands set aside specifically for fish and wildlife. The majority of these lands, 77 million acres, are in Alaska. The remaining acres are spread across the other 49 states and several United States territories. In addition to refuges, the Service manages thousands of small wetlands, national fish hatcheries, 64 fishery resource offices, and 78 ecological services field stations. The Service enforces federal wildlife laws, administers the Endangered Species Act, manages migratory bird populations, restores nationally significant fisheries, conserves and restores wildlife habitat, and helps foreign governments with their conservation efforts. It also oversees the Federal Aid program that distributes hundreds of millions of dollars in excise taxes on fishing and hunting equipment to state fish and wildlife agencies.

NATIONAL WILDLIFE REFUGE SYSTEM

The mission of the National Wildlife Refuge System, as defined by the National Wildlife Refuge System Improvement Act of 1997 is:

"...to administer a national network of lands and waters for the conservation, management, and where appropriate, restoration of the fish, wildlife and plant resources and their habitats within the United States for the benefit of present and future generations of Americans."

The National Wildlife Refuge System Improvement Act of 1997 established, for the first time, a clear legislative mission of wildlife conservation for the National Wildlife Refuge System. Actions were initiated in 1997 to comply with the direction of this new legislation, including an effort to complete comprehensive conservation plans for all refuges. These plans, which are completed with full public involvement, help guide the management of refuges by establishing natural resources and recreation/education programs. Consistent with this Act, approved plans will serve as the guidelines for refuge management for the next 15 years. The Act states that each refuge shall be managed to:

- Fulfill the mission of the National Wildlife Refuge System;
- Fulfill the individual purposes of each refuge;
- Consider the needs of wildlife first;
- Fulfill requirements of comprehensive conservation plans that are prepared for each unit of the Refuge System;
- Maintain the biological integrity, diversity, and environmental health of the Refuge System; and
- Recognize that wildlife-dependent recreation activities, including hunting, fishing, wildlife observation, wildlife photography, and environmental education and interpretation, are legitimate and priority public uses; and allow refuge managers authority to determine compatible public uses.

Approximately 38 million people visited national wildlife refuges in 2002, most to observe wildlife in their natural habitats. As the number of visitors grows, there are significant economic benefits to local communities. In 2001, 82 million people, 16 years and older, either fished, hunted, or observed wildlife, generating $108 billion. In a study completed in 2002 on 15 refuges, visitation had grown 36 percent in 7 years. At the same time, the number of jobs generated in surrounding communities grew to 120 per refuge, up from 87 jobs in 1995, pouring more than $2.2 million into local economies. The 15 refuges in the study were Chincoteague (Virginia); National Elk (Wyoming); Crab Orchard (Illinois); Eufaula (Alabama); Charles M. Russell (Montana); Umatilla (Oregon); Quivira (Kansas); Mattamuskeet (North Carolina); Upper Souris (North Dakota); San Francisco Bay (California); Laguna Atacosa (Texas); Horicon (Wisconsin); Las Vegas (Nevada); Tule Lake (California); and Tensas River (Louisiana) – the same refuges identified for the 1995 study. Other findings also validate the belief that communities near refuges benefit economically. Expenditures on food, lodging, and transportation grew to $6.8 million per refuge, up 31 percent from $5.2 million in 1995. For each federal dollar spent on the Refuge System, surrounding communities benefited with $4.43 in recreation expenditures and $1.42 in job-related income (Caudill and Laughland, unpubl. data).

Volunteers continue to be a major contributor to the success of the Refuge System. In 2002, volunteers contributed more than 1.5 million hours on refuges nationwide, a service valued at more than $22 million.

The wildlife and habitat vision for national wildlife refuges stresses that wildlife comes first; that ecosystems, biodiversity, and wilderness are vital concepts in refuge management; that refuges must be healthy and growth must be strategic; and that the Refuge System serves as a model for habitat management with broad participation from others.

LEGAL POLICY CONTEXT

Administration of national wildlife refuges is guided by the mission and goals of the National Wildlife Refuge System, congressional legislation, Presidential executive orders, and international treaties. Policies for management options of refuges are further refined by administrative guidelines established by the Secretary of the Interior and by policy guidelines established by the Director of the Fish and Wildlife Service. Refer to Appendix B for a complete listing of relevant legal mandates.

Lands within the National Wildlife Refuge System are closed to public use unless specifically and legally opened. All programs and uses must be evaluated based on mandates set forth in the National Wildlife Refuge System Improvement Act. Those mandates are to:

- Contribute to ecosystem goals, as well as refuge purposes and goals;
- Conserve, manage, and restore fish, wildlife, and plant resources and their habitats;
- Monitor the trends of fish, wildlife, and plants;
- Manage and ensure appropriate visitor uses as those uses benefit the conservation of fish and wildlife resources and contribute to the enjoyment of the public (these uses include hunting, fishing, wildlife observation, wildlife photography, and environmental education and interpretation); and
- Ensure that visitor activities are compatible with refuge purposes.

NATIONAL AND INTERNATIONAL CONSERVATION PLANS AND INITIATIVES

Multiple partnerships have been developed among government and private entities to address the environmental problems affecting regions. There is a large amount of conservation and protection information that defines the role of the refuge at the local, national, international, and ecosystem levels. Conservation initiatives include broad-scale planning and cooperation between affected parties to address declining trends of natural, physical, social, and economic environments. The conservation guidance described below, along with issues, problems and trends, was reviewed and integrated where appropriate into this final comprehensive conservation plan.

Perhaps the greatest need of the Service is communication with the public and public agency participation in efforts to carry out the mission of the National Wildlife Refuge System. Many agencies, organizations, institutions, and businesses have developed relationships with the Service to advance the mission of national wildlife refuges. This final comprehensive conservation plan supports, among others, the Partners in Flight Plan, the North American Waterfowl Management Plan, the Western Hemisphere Shorebird Reserve Network, and the National Wetlands Priority Conservation Plan.

NORTH AMERICAN BIRD CONSERVATION INITIATIVE

The North American Bird Conservation Initiative is a coalition of government, private and academic organizations, and private industry leaders addressing bird conservation. The initiative's vision is to achieve regionally based, biologically driven, landscape-oriented partnerships that deliver the full spectrum of bird conservation across the North American continent and that support simultaneous, on-the-ground delivery of conservation for all birds. As a result, North American bird populations will flourish, because they are valued by society, including all levels of government and private initiative.

NORTH AMERICAN WATERFOWL MANAGEMENT PLAN

The North American Waterfowl Management Plan is an international action plan to conserve migratory birds throughout the continent. The plan's goal is to return waterfowl populations to the levels of the 1970s by conserving wetland and upland habitat. Canada and the United States signed the plan in 1986 in reaction to critically low numbers of waterfowl. Mexico joined in 1994, making it a truly continental effort. The plan is a partnership of federal, provincial/state, and municipal governments, non-governmental organizations, private companies and many individuals, all working towards achieving better wetland habitat for the benefit of migratory birds, other wetland-associated species, and people.

PARTNERS IN FLIGHT BIRD CONSERVATION PLAN

The Partners in Flight Bird Conservation Plan was launched in 1990 in response to growing concerns about many land bird species. It is a cooperative effort involving partnerships among federal, state, and local governments, philanthropic foundations, conservation organizations, professional organization, industry, the academic community, and private individuals. The central premise of Partners in Flight has been that resources of public and private organizations in North and South America must be combined, coordinated, and increased in order to achieve success in conserving land bird populations in this Hemisphere.

U.S. SHOREBIRD CONSERVATION PLAN

The U.S. Shorebird Conservation Plan is a partnership effort throughout the United States to ensure that stable and self-sustaining populations of shorebird species are restored and protected. The plan was developed by a wide range of agencies, organizations, and shorebird experts for separate regions of the country, and identifies conservation goals, critical habitat conservation needs, key research needs, and proposed education and outreach programs to increase awareness of shorebirds and the threats they face.

NORTH AMERICAN WATERBIRD CONSERVATION PLAN

This plan provides a framework for the conservation and management of 210 species of waterbirds in 29 nations. Threats to waterbird populations include destruction of inland and coastal wetlands, introduced predators and invasive species, pollutants, mortality from fisheries and industries, disturbance, and conflicts arising from abundant species. Particularly important habitats of the southeast region include pelagic areas, marshes, forested wetlands, and barrier and sea island complexes. Fifteen species of waterbirds are federally listed, including breeding populations of wood storks, Mississippi sandhill cranes, whooping cranes, interior least terns, and gulf coast populations of brown pelicans. A key objective of this plan is the standardization of data collection efforts to better recommend effective conservation measures.

U.S. WOODCOCK PLAN

The U.S. Woodcock Plan was written by the Service in 1990 to "guide the conservation of woodcock in the United States." Although no step-down plans have been written, the plan gives general guidance for habitat population management at the national level.

RELATIONSHIP TO STATE WILDLIFE AGENCY

A provision of the National Wildlife Refuge System Improvement Act of 1997, and subsequent agency policy, is that the Service shall ensure timely and effective cooperation and collaboration with other state fish and game agencies and tribal governments during the course of acquiring and managing refuges. State wildlife management areas and national wildlife refuges provide the foundation for the protection of species, and contribute to the overall health and sustainment of fish and wildlife species in the State of Louisiana.

The Louisiana Department of Wildlife and Fisheries (http://www.wlf.state.la.vs) is a state-partnering agency with the Service, charged with enforcement responsibilities for migratory birds and endangered species, as well as managing the State's natural resources. It also manages approximately 1.4 million acres of coastal marshes and wildlife management areas in Louisiana. The Department of Wildlife and Fisheries coordinates the state's wildlife conservation program and provides public recreation opportunities, including an extensive hunting and fishing program, on several wildlife management areas located near Grand Cote Refuge (e.g., Grassy Lake, Pomme de Terre, Red River, Spring Bayou, and Three Rivers). The Department of Wildlife and Fisheries' participation and contribution throughout this comprehensive conservation planning process has been valuable, and it is continuing its work with the Service to provide ongoing opportunities for an open dialogue with the public to improve the ecological sustainment of fish and wildlife in Louisiana. Not only has the Department participated in biological reviews, public scoping meetings, and field reviews as part of the planning process, it also is an active partner in annual hunt coordination planning, and various wildlife and habitat surveys. In the past two years, Grand Cote Refuge has initiated hunting opportunities for rabbits, deer, waterfowl, doves, wild turkey, and feral hogs in cooperation with the Louisiana Department of Wildlife and Fisheries.

II. Refuge Overview

INTRODUCTION

Grand Cote National Wildlife Refuge is in west-central Avoyelles Parish, Louisiana, about 10 miles west of the city of Marksville (population 6,087) and 20 miles southeast of the city of Alexandria (population 46,000), south of Highway 1, west of Highway 115, and north and east of Highway 114. The refuge is part of the Central Louisiana National Wildlife Refuge Complex, which includes Grand Cote, Lake Ophelia, and Cat Island Refuges (Figure 1). The refuge covers 6,075 acres. An additional 6,925 acres of land are included in the approved acquisition boundary of the refuge (Figure 2). The refuge was established in 1989 to provide wintering habitat for mallards, pintails, blue-winged teal, and wood ducks, and production habitat for wood ducks to meet the goals of the North American Waterfowl Management Plan.

Grand Cote Refuge is a natural sump that is bordered by the higher ridge lands of the Red River on the north and east and by the terrace uplands on the west and south. The refuge is dissected by two water bodies, Choctaw Bayou and Coulee des Grues. Currently, the refuge provides a mix of various habitat types, including moist-soil waterfowl impoundments, cropland "hot food" waterfowl impoundments, remnant pieces of mature bottomland hardwood forests, reforested areas, cypress sloughs, and upland forests. Many species of migratory birds, resident birds, mammals, fish, and other wildlife utilize these habitats.

REFUGE HISTORY AND PURPOSE

Grand Cote National Wildlife Refuge was established in 1989 under the authority of the Fish and Wildlife Act of 1956, which calls for:

> "...the development, advancement, management, conservation, and protection of fish and wildlife resources...." [16 USC 742f(a)(4)];

Under the authority of the Emergency Wetlands Resources Act of 1986, which calls for:

> "the conservation of the wetlands of the Nation in order to maintain the public benefits they provide and to help fulfill international obligations contained in various migratory bird treaties and conventions...." (16 USC 3901 (b), 100 Stat. 3583);

and under the authority of the Migratory Bird Conservation Act as amended in 1989, which calls for:

> "...use as an inviolate sanctuary, or any other management purpose, for migratory birds." (USC 715d);

With these establishing authorities, purposes for Grand Cote Refuge were further identified in the 1993 Environmental Assessment, Finding of No Significant Impact, and Land Protection Plan prepared by the Service for the following:

- Provide wintering habitat for mallards, pintails, blue-winged teal, and wood ducks;

- Provide production habitat for wood ducks to meet the goals of the North American Waterfowl Management Plan.

Figure 1. The location of Central Louisiana National Wildlife Refuge Complex in Avoyelles Parish, Louisiana

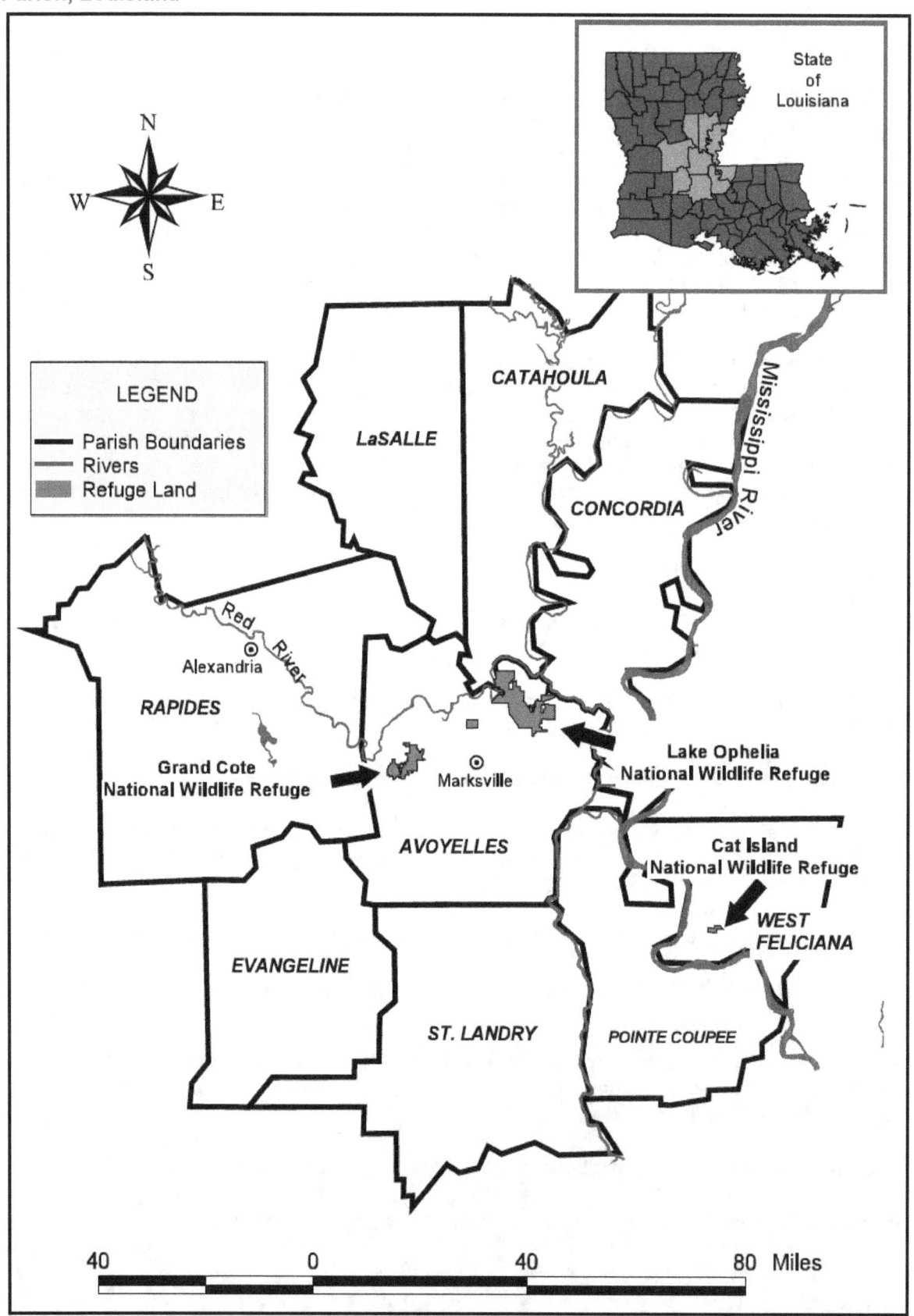

Figure 2. Current and approved acquisition boundary of Grand Cote National Wildlife Refuge

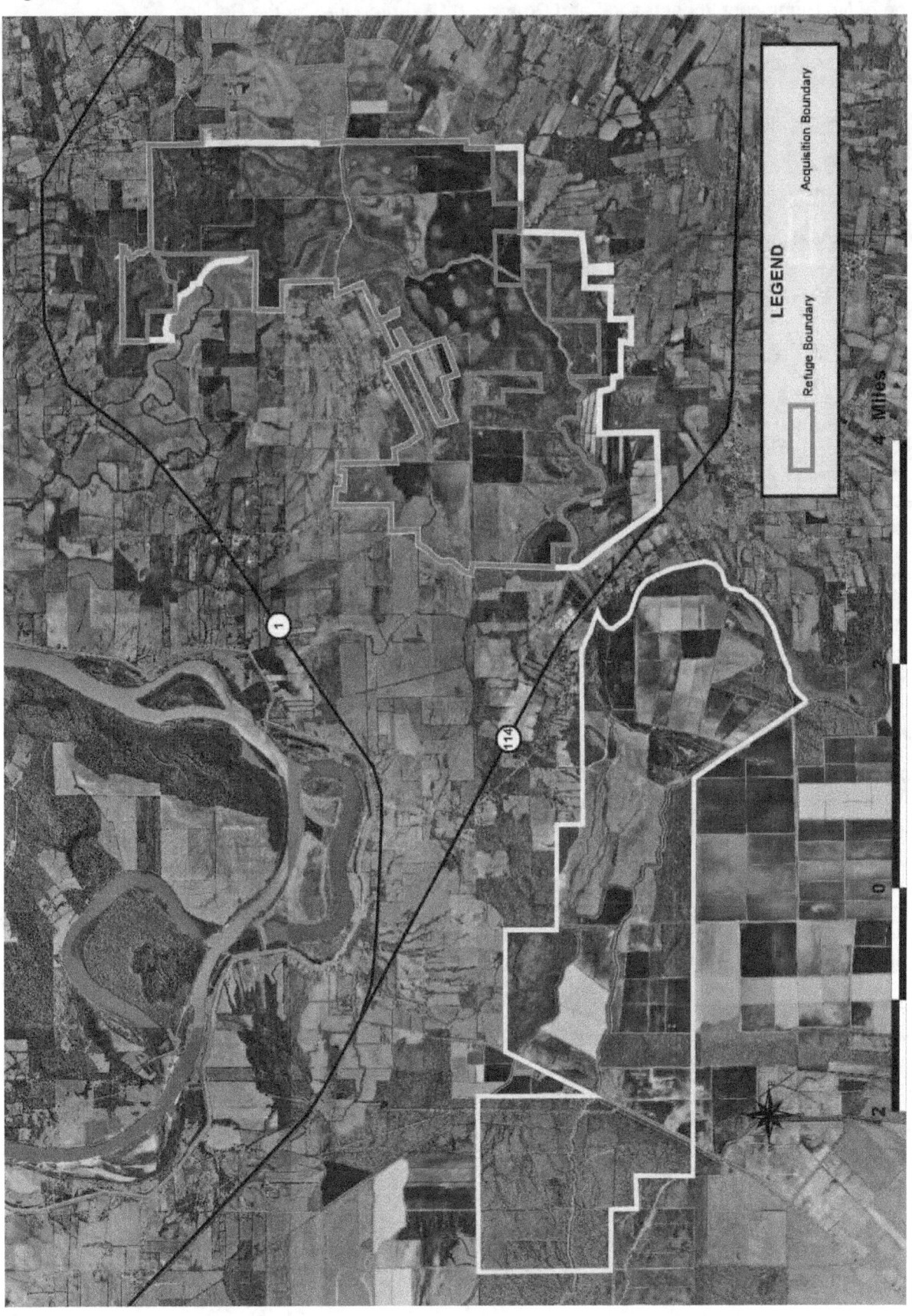

The following secondary purposes were further identified in the 1993 Environmental Assessment, Finding of No Significant Impact, and Land Protection Plan prepared by the Service:

- Provide habitat for threatened and endangered species;

- Provide habitat for a natural diversity of plant and wildlife species; and

- Provide opportunities for wildlife-oriented recreation and environmental education when compatible with other refuge objectives.

SPECIAL DESIGNATIONS

WILDERNESS REVIEW

Currently, there are no areas of special designation on Grand Cote Refuge. However, refuge planning policy requires a wilderness review as part of the comprehensive conservation planning process. The Wilderness Act of 1964 defines a wilderness area as an area of federal land that retains its primeval character and influence, without permanent improvements or human inhabitation, and is managed so as to preserve its natural conditions and which 1) generally appears to have been influenced primarily by the forces of nature, with the imprint of man's work substantially unnoticeable; 2) has outstanding opportunities for solitude or primitive and unconfined type of recreation; 3) has at least 5,000 contiguous roadless acres, or is of sufficient size to make practicable its preservation and use in an unimpeded condition, or is a roadless island regardless of size; 4) does not substantially exhibit the effects of logging, farming, grazing, or other extensive development or alteration of the landscape or its wilderness character could be restored through appropriate management at the time of review; and 5) may contain ecological, geological, or other features of scientific, educational, scenic, or historic value.

The lands within Grand Cote Refuge were reviewed for their suitability in meeting the criteria for wilderness, as defined by the Wilderness Act of 1964. No lands in the refuge were found to meet these criteria. Therefore, the suitability of refuge lands for wilderness designation is not further analyzed in this plan.

ECOSYSTEM CONTEXT

The refuge lies within a physiographic region known as the Mississippi Alluvial Valley (MAV) (Figure 3). The MAV was at one time a 25-million-acre forested wetland complex that extended along both sides of the Mississippi River from the State of Illinois to the State of Louisiana. Although the refuge was part of this very productive bottomland hardwood ecosystem, most of the forest on and around the refuge was cleared in the late 1960s for agricultural production or developed for rural homesites. Since this land was cleared, most of the refuge has been under intensive rice production, so there is an extensive system of man-made levees, irrigation ditches, and water control structures. Due to this infrastructure, the refuge is capable of providing critical shallow-water habitat for migratory waterfowl and shorebirds.

Figure 3. Mississippi Alluvial Valley

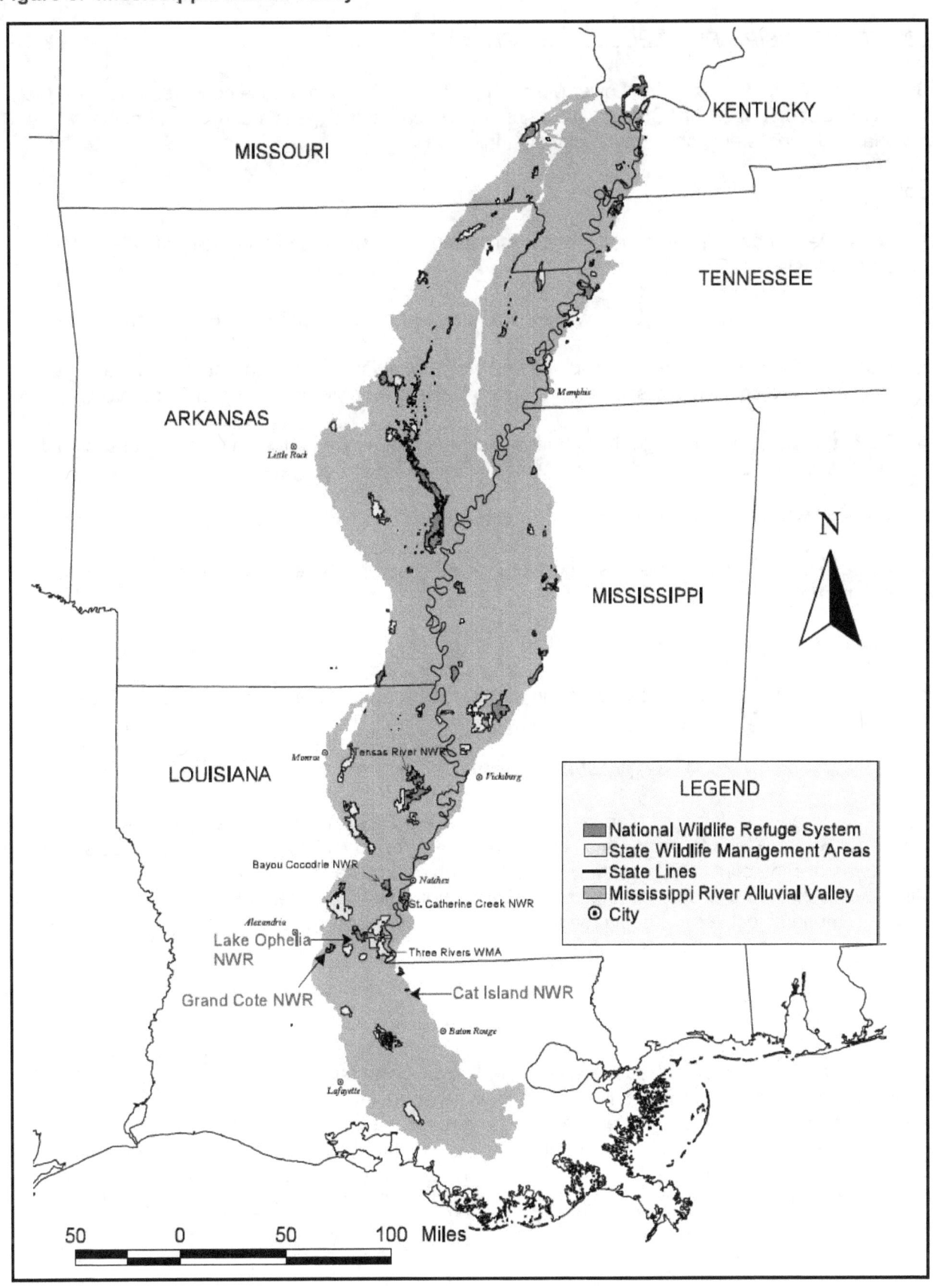

REGIONAL CONSERVATION PLANS AND INITIATIVES

LOWER MISSISSIPPI RIVER ECOSYSTEM PLAN

Grand Cote Refuge is part of the Lower Mississippi River Ecosystem and is considered to be in the West Gulf Coastal Plain Bird Conservation Area. As such, the refuge is a component of many regional and ecosystem conservation planning initiatives.

Goals:

1. Conserve, enhance, protect, and monitor migratory bird populations and their habitats in the Lower Mississippi River Ecosystem.

2. Protect, restore, and manage the wetlands of the Lower Mississippi River Ecosystem.

3. Protect and/or restore imperiled habitats and viable populations of all threatened, endangered, and candidate species and species of concern in the Lower Mississippi River Ecosystem.

4. Protect, restore, and manage the fisheries and other aquatic resources historically associated with the wetlands and waters of the Lower Mississippi River Ecosystem.

5. Restore, manage, and protect national wildlife refuges and national fish hatcheries.

6. Increase public awareness and support for Lower Mississippi River Ecosystem resources and their management.

7. Enforce natural resource laws.

8. Protect, restore, and enhance water and air quality throughout the Lower Mississippi River Ecosystem.

NORTH AMERICAN WATERFOWL MANAGEMENT PLAN

The North American Waterfowl Management Plan (NAWMP) is an international agreement among the United States, Canada, and Mexico to increase waterfowl populations by restoring crucial wetland habitats across the continent. Currently, step-down objectives have been developed for the Mississippi Alluvial Valley through the Lower Mississippi Valley Joint Venture cooperative effort; however, these objectives are being refined by the NAWMP Management Board and will continue to be incorporated into regional planning for the refuge.

PARTNERS IN FLIGHT

Partners in Flight, a cooperative effort involving partnerships among federal, state, and local governments and other organizations, has formed Bird Conservation Plans by Bird Conservation Regions that set conservation priorities and habitat and population objectives. Fragmentation of bottomland hardwood forests has left many of the remaining small forested tracts on Grand Cote Refuge surrounded by a sea of agricultural lands. Although the refuge is not considered a priority bird conservation area, the small remnant habitat and associated bird species that are considered a priority in the West Gulf Coastal Plain include the white-eyed vireo, yellow-billed cuckoo, and red-headed woodpecker.

U.S. SHOREBIRD CONSERVATION PLAN

The U.S. Shorebird Conservation Plan is a partnership effort being undertaken throughout the country to ensure that shorebird populations are restored and protected. Primary objectives of this plan are:

1. Develop a scientifically sound monitoring system to provide practical information to researchers and land managers.

2. Identify principles upon which management plans can integrate shorebird habitat conservation with multiple species strategies.

3. Design a strategy for increasing public awareness and information concerning wetlands and shorebirds.

Grand Cote Refuge is included in the Lower Mississippi/Western Gulf Coast Shorebird Planning Region and Bird Conservation Region. This plan recommends that public lands provide as much fall shorebird habitat as possible to meet the goal (520 hectare) of fall habitat in Louisiana. The refuge is considered an important shorebird area, with the following species considered high priority for the region: piping plover, American golden-plover, marbled godwit, ruddy turnstone, red knot, sanderling, buff-breasted sandpiper, American woodcock, and Wilson's phalarope.

NORTH AMERICAN BIRD CONSERVATION INITIATIVE

Started in 1999, the North American Bird Conservation Initiative is a coalition of government agencies, private organizations, academic institutions, and private industry leaders in the United States, Canada, and Mexico, working to ensure the long-term health of North America's native bird populations by fostering an integrated approach to bird conservation to benefit all birds in all habitats. The four international and national bird initiatives include the North American Waterfowl Management Plan, Partners in Flight, Waterbird Conservation for the Americas, and the U.S. Shorebird Conservation Plan. The combined effectiveness of these separate programs exceeds the total of their parts.

U.S. WOODCOCK PLAN

The U.S. Woodcock Plan was written by the Service in 1990 to "guide the conservation of woodcock in the United States." Although no step-down plans have been written, the plan gives general guidance for habitat population management at the national level.

ECOLOGICAL THREATS AND PROBLEMS

FOREST LOSS AND FRAGMENTATION

The Mississippi Alluvial Valley has changed markedly over the last 100 years as civilization spread throughout the area. From the 1950s to the 1990s, it has been estimated that 20 million acres of bottomland hardwood forested wetlands have been lost (Figure 4). The greatest changes to the landscape have been in the form of land clearing for agricultural and flood control projects.

Figure 4. Forest cover changes in the Mississippi Alluvial Valley

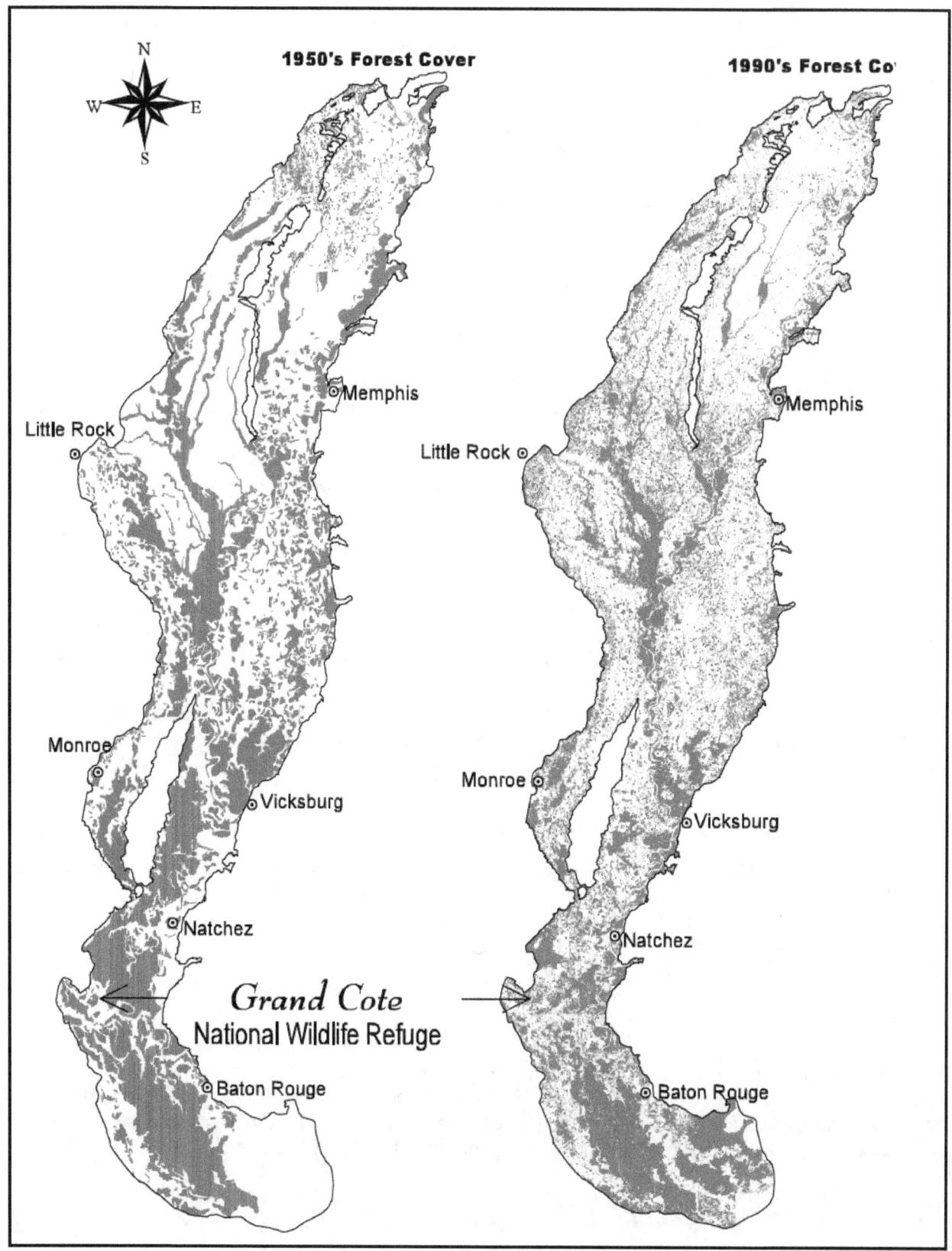

Although these changes have allowed people to settle and earn a living in the area, they have had a tremendous effect on biological diversity and integrity, and environmental health of the Mississippi Alluvial Valley. Vast areas of bottomland hardwood forests have been reduced to forest fragments, ranging in size from very small tracts of limited functional value to a few large areas that have maintained many of the original functions and values of forested wetlands. This process, which is known as forest fragmentation, has reduced the size and connectivity of forest habitat patches and resulted in the disruption of extensive forest habitats into smaller and smaller isolated patches. Severe forest fragmentation has resulted in a significant decline in biological diversity and integrity. Species endemic to the Mississippi Alluvial Valley that have become extinct, threatened or endangered include the red wolf, Florida panther, ivory-billed woodpecker, Bachman's warbler, and Louisiana black bear.

Breeding bird surveys show continuing declines in species and species population numbers. The avian species most adversely affected by forest fragmentation include those that are area-sensitive (i.e., dependent on large continuous blocks of hardwood forest); those that depend on forest interiors; those that have special habitat requirements, such as mature forests or a particular food source; and those that require good water quality.

More than 70 species of breeding migratory birds are found in the region. Some of these species, including Swainson's warbler, prothonotary warbler, swallow-tailed kites, wood thrush, and cerulean warbler, have declined significantly and need the benefits of large forested blocks to recover and sustain their existence.

Due to fragmentation, the forest edge and the brown-headed cowbird (i.e., a seed-eating bird common in agricultural areas) are now closer to the natural nesting sites of many forest interior-nesting birds. The brown-headed cowbird is a parasitic nester that lays eggs in the nests of other birds, rather than building a nest of its own. Nestling cowbirds often out-compete host species, because the cowbirds are typically larger and more aggressive. This results in poor reproductive success and declining populations of forest interior-nesting species.

Fragmentation of bottomland hardwood forests has left many of the remaining forested tracts surrounded by agricultural lands. Intensive agriculture has removed most of the forested corridors along sloughs that formerly connected the forest patches. The loss of connectivity between the remaining forested areas hinders the movement of wildlife between tracts, and reduces the functional values of many remaining smaller forest tracts. The lost connections also result in a loss of gene flow. Restoring the connections to allow gene flow and reestablish travel corridors is particularly important for some wide-ranging species, such as the threatened Louisiana black bear.

ALTERATIONS TO HYDROLOGY

In addition to the loss of a vast acreage of bottomland hardwood forested wetlands, there have been significant alterations in the region's hydrology due to urban development, river channel modification, flood control levees, reservoirs, and deforestation, as well as degradation of aquatic systems from excessive sedimentation and contaminants.

The natural hydrology of a region is directly responsible for the connectedness of forested wetlands and indirectly responsible for the complexity and diversity of habitats through its effects on topography and soils. Natural resource managers recognize the importance of dynamic hydrology to forested wetlands and waterfowl-habitat relationships (Fredrickson and Heitmeyer 1988).

Large-scale, man-made hydrological alterations have changed the natural spatial and temporal patterns of flooding throughout the entire Mississippi Alluvial Valley. In addition, these alterations have reduced both the extent and the duration of annual seasonal flooding. The loss of this annual flooding regime has had a tremendous effect on the forested wetlands and their associated wetland-dependent species.

In view of the hydrologic changes, it is very difficult—if not impossible—to fully emulate and reconstruct the structure and functions of a natural wetland. According to Mitsch and Gosselink (1993), restoration of wetland functions is especially difficult since wetlands depend on a dynamic interface of hydrologic regimes to maintain water, vegetation, and animal complexes and processes.

SILTATION OF AQUATIC ECOSYSTEMS

Aquatic systems, including lakes, rivers, sloughs and bayous, have been degraded as a result of deforestation and hydrologic alteration. Clearing of bottomland hardwood forests has led to an accelerated accumulation of sediments and contaminants in all aquatic systems. Many water bodies are now filled with sediments, which greatly reduce their surface area and depth. Concurrently, the non-point source runoff of excess nutrients and contaminants is threatening the area's remaining aquatic resources. In Louisiana, the Service lists one fish species as threatened and one as endangered.

Hydrologic alterations have basically eliminated the geomorphological processes that created oxbow lakes, sloughs, and river meander scars. Consequently, the protection, conservation, and restoration of these aquatic resources take on an added importance in light of the alterations associated with flood control and navigation.

PROLIFERATION OF INVASIVE AQUATIC PLANTS

Compounding the problems faced by aquatic systems is the growing threat from invasive aquatic vegetation. Static water levels caused by the lack of annual flooding, and reduced water depths resulting from excessive sedimentation, have created conditions favorable for the establishment and proliferation of several species of invasive aquatic plants. Additionally, the introduction of exotic (nonnative) vegetation capable of aggressive growth is further threatening viability of aquatic systems. These invasive aquatic species threaten the natural aquatic vegetation important to aquatic systems, and choke waterways to a degree that often prevents recreational use.

PHYSICAL RESOURCES

CLIMATE

The climate at the refuge is humid subtropical and is primarily influenced by the refuge's subtropical latitude and proximity to the Gulf of Mexico. The climate is controlled by two principal air masses. Warm, moist air from the Gulf of Mexico generally dominates in the spring and summer, and cooler, drier air from the Central Plains prevails during the winter months. Extended hot, sultry summers and moderately cool winters are the norm.

The average annual air temperature is 65 degrees Fahrenheit. During winter, the average temperature is 50 degrees, with an average daily minimum of 39 degrees. Average seasonal snowfall is less than one inch. The average temperature is 81 degrees during the summer (Martin 1986), but temperatures above 90 degrees occur almost daily.

The mean annual precipitation is 60 inches. Half of this rainfall (30 inches) usually falls during April through September. The growing season is about 235 days long and begins in mid-March and ends during early November. Thunderstorms occur on average about 70 days each year, with most occurring during the summer months. The average relative humidity in the mid-afternoon is about 60 percent. Humidity is higher at night, with the average at dawn being 90 percent (Martin 1986).

The sun shines 60 percent of the time during the summer, and 50 percent during winter. Prevailing wind is from the south. Average wind speed is highest, 9 miles per hour, during the spring months. These climatic values play an important role in influencing the area's hydrologic regime, which subsequently shapes ecosystem processes and functions.

GEOLOGY AND TOPOGRAPHY

As the climate changed on the earth, marine and deltaic sediments have been deposited in alternating cycles in Louisiana. Geologists have determined from studying these deposits that a major river system, corresponding to the modern Mississippi River, has persisted here at least since the Gulf of Mexico began to form (Louisiana Geologic Survey 1990).

The Tertiary period, which extended from 65 to 1.8 million years ago, began with a warming trend where the sea covered almost the entire Lower Red River Basin. In the early Eocene epoch, which began about 54 million years ago, the land began to build up again as the continental ice sheets advanced. However, this trend was reversed during the late Eocene when a second advancement of the sea occurred. With the sea as far inland as Natchitoches Parish, the last cycle began in the early Oligocene Epoch (38 to 23 million years ago). In Miocene time (23 to 5 million years ago), the sea level dropped and sedimentation began to extend the land gulfward (U.S. Army Corps of Engineers 1975).

The refuge lies within the Mississippi Alluvial Plain section of the Coastal Plain Province (Beccasio et al. 1983), to the west of the confluence of the Mississippi and Red Rivers in Avoyelles Parish. The topography of the refuge has been greatly influenced by the aggrading Mississippi and Red Rivers, and much of the geology is from Quaternary (1.8 million years ago to present) alluvial deposits. Although the continental ice sheets did not reach this far south, the Lower Mississippi Valley carried glacial meltwaters and outwash in a braided-stream pattern that concurrently widened and aggraded the valley during periods of waning glaciation. As each glacial cycle progressed, the Red River abandoned its braided stream configuration in favor of a single-channel meandering pattern. This alluvium has been sorted, reworked, and deposited many times by riverine processes.

During flood periods prior to human influence, stream channels within the Mississippi Alluvial Valley, unable to hold the complete volume of water within their banks, overtopped and spilled onto adjacent floodplains. In doing so, the velocity of these sediment-laden waters decreased dramatically. Unable to continue to carry their bedload, these waters dropped the coarsest particles closest to the stream channel and the finer particles farther away. These deposits formed natural levees, which gained elevation closer to the river channel.

Another result of this localized deposition was the creation of lowlands at the foot of these natural levees, which received only the clay particles held in suspension in flood waters (Fisk 1940). These lowlands paralleled the meander belt of the stream for great distances and were utilized as seasonal backwater flood storage areas. Water within the channel would continue to erode the banks, and often would cut through these natural levees. The stream would then change its course and occupy the lowland channel.

The formations of alluvium described above comprise the entire Grand Cote Refuge. Relict channels and natural levees are often referred to as ridge and swale topography. Human disturbances, including the construction of artificial levees and channelization projects, have drastically altered these natural alluvial processes within the Mississippi and Red River floodplains.

SOILS

The soils at the refuge demonstrate the influence that the Mississippi and Red Rivers have had on the terrain. The refuge contains mostly hydric soils that fall into four broad series of soil groups. The dominant soil series on the refuge are the following:

Latanier Clay - level, somewhat poorly drained soil in intermediate positions on the neutral levees of the Red River and its tributaries.

Moreland Clay - level, somewhat poorly drained soil in low positions on the natural levees of the Red River and its tributaries.

Moreland Clay occasionally flooded - level, somewhat poorly drained soil in low positions on the natural levees of the Red River and its tributaries.

Solier Clay - level, somewhat poorly drained soil on low stream terraces.

HYDROLOGY

The nature of the Mississippi River in pre-modern times was one of a dynamic and changing system. The many courses the river has taken in recent geologic history have been noted by geologists. Fisk (1940) wrote:

> *The youngest pre-modern course of the Mississippi River is the most easily interpreted; it can be traced along the Tensas River in northeastern Louisiana southward to Black River. Black River and Tensas River, which locally reverse the original drainage direction, unite and drain southeastward through a crevasse channel. Red River enters this meander belt in another crevasse channel opening. South of the Red River, the meander is occupied by Lake Long and Bayou des Glaises and continues to the Atchafalaya River, which follow an old meander from Lower Old River, a recent Mississippi cut-off meander, to Simmesport.*

Two distinct aquifer systems underlie Avoyelles Parish: the Quaternary and the upper Tertiary. The water levels in both of these aquifer systems are generally less than 50 feet below the surface. The Quaternary aquifer can supply very large quantities of fresh water to parish residents. The Quaternary aquifer is composed of poorly sorted sand and gravel. It ranges in thickness from 50 to 150 feet. This aquifer offers the greatest potential source of ground water. Water in this aquifer is generally suitable for irrigation, but its hardness and high iron content must be treated for most other uses (Martin 1986).

Beneath this aquifer is the upper Tertiary system, which can yield moderate to large supplies of fresh water in the Bunkie-Hessmer and Simmesport-Odenburg areas (Marie 1971). This aquifer system is recharged principally by rainfall. In areas where the aquifer system has been developed for public and industrial supplies, withdrawals from wells have lowered the water level as much as 20 feet (Marie 1971). Aquifers in this system range from 20 to 80 feet in thickness and are composed principally of well-sorted, fine- to medium-grained sand (Martin 1986).

Grand Cote Refuge is a natural sump that is bordered by the higher ridge lands of the Red River on the north and east and by the terrace uplands on the west and south. The refuge is dissected by two water bodies: Choctaw Bayou and Coulee des Grues. Choctaw Bayou is an outlet for the Chatlain Lake Canal, which provides drainage for the city of Alexandria and other areas north of the refuge. During significant rainfall events, water from the Chatlain Lake Canal causes backwater flooding onto the refuge via Choctaw Bayou and Coulee des Grues.

Prior to its establishment, the area encompassing the refuge was intensively farmed, and a series of man-made levees, irrigation ditches, pumps, and water control structures were constructed to facilitate farming. Most of those structures are still present on the refuge today, and are used to manage water levels for waterfowl and shorebirds. The natural hydrology of the area, however, has been altered by those structures. In addition to the structures above, the refuge uses laser land leveling on some cooperatively farmed fields, which produces uniform topography, and influences hydrology. Removal of, or modifications to, some of those structures may reestablish more natural hydrologic regimes onto portions of the area; however, those modifications could impact other refuge management currently in place, such as cooperative farming for waterfowl, shorebird, and wading bird management.

WATER QUALITY AND QUANTITY

Historically, the water quality of the refuge has not been monitored. Water quality within the Red River north of the refuge has been affected by mercury contamination from an unknown source (Louisiana Department of Environmental Quality 1998).

Recently, Grand Cote Refuge was one of 26 refuges in the Mississippi Alluvial Valley surveyed for chemical contamination. Samples of water, sediment, and fish were collected, and passive sampling devices were deployed. Residues of current-use pesticides, organochlorine pesticides, polychlorinated biphenyls, polycyclic aromatic hydrocarbons, and mercury were measured along with limited toxicity testing (Shea et al. 2001). Grand Cote Refuge had one of the lowest levels of chemical contamination of all refuges surveyed. Although each of the chemical contaminants surveyed for was detected at the refuge, none were detected at levels of concern to human health or fish/wildlife.

The Environmental Protection Agency's *Index of Watershed Indicators* shows that 80 to 100 percent of the water bodies within this area of the lower Red River watershed are meeting designated uses, and they characterize the streams in this area as having overall better water quality and a low vulnerability to problems related to runoff. The Environmental Protection Agency has identified a moderate loss of wetlands in this watershed. Wetlands perform many important functions, such as improving water quality, recharging groundwater, providing natural flood control, and supporting a wide variety of fish, wildlife, and plants. The economic importance of wetlands to commercial fisheries and recreational use is also known to be significant. Land clearing, man-made levees, navigation structures, stream channelization projects, and canal and ditch construction have impaired the historic functions of forested wetlands.

Prior to the 1960s, the area that is now Grand Cote Refuge was a large, bottomland hardwood swamp. The Choctaw Bayou, which bisects the refuge, is the main drainage system for several areas to the north, including the city of Alexandria. The Choctaw Bayou frequently backs up after a major rainfall event, causing backwater flooding on most of the refuge because of its slight relief and sump-like nature. When the land was cleared, an extensive set of levees were constructed to protect farm fields from flooding. These levees still protect farm fields during specific times of the year, but also serve as a means to capture flood water and maximize shallow-water habitat.

Flood control measures off-refuge, including the Chatlain Lake Canal and the Red River levee system, have impacted historic hydrologic regimes. Extensive land clearing for agriculture off-refuge has also increased sediment, nutrient, and contaminant inputs into Choctaw Bayou and Coulee des Grues, and into other water bodies located outside of the refuge. Additionally, a cannery located adjacent to the refuge may discharge effluent periodically.

The U.S. Army Corps of Engineers, Vicksburg District, and the Avoyelles Parish Police Jury are currently investigating potential solutions to water quality problems experienced in the Spring Bayou area of the parish. This area lies east of the refuge and receives inputs from Coulee des Grues. The Corps has developed several alternatives to address Spring Bayou's water quality problems. The alternative preferred by the Police Jury includes: installing an inlet structure through the Red River levee at Choctaw Bayou along with a pump to reestablish flows from the Red River into the Spring Bayou area; controlling structures on Bayou du Lac and Coulee des Grues to reduce sediment inputs into the Spring Bayou area; clearing and snagging the channels in Choctaw Bayou and Coulee des Grues; dredging portions of several water bodies located outside the refuge for flow conveyance; and modifying an existing weir. Those actions listed above have the potential for direct and indirect impacts on the refuge's hydrology and water quality. Water quality would be expected to improve with reintroduction of Red River inputs. The amount and frequency of backwater flooding on the refuge could be altered by the proposed control structure on Coulee des Grues, and by downstream dredging. The Feasibility Cost Sharing Agreement to conduct the feasibility study was signed on June 15, 2006. The study should be completed in June 2009.

A thorough analysis of existing hydrology on the refuge is necessary in order to predict the impacts of aquatic restoration or flood-control actions proposed by this project. The Service intends to support this project and fully participate with the principal partners.

BIOLOGICAL RESOURCES

HABITAT

Grand Cote Refuge is a natural sump that is bordered by the higher ridge lands of the Red River on the north and east and by the terrace uplands on the west and south. The refuge is dissected by two water bodies--Choctaw Bayou and Coulee des Grues. Currently, the refuge provides a mix of various habitat types, including small remnant pieces of mature bottomland hardwood forests, reforested areas, upland hardwood forests, waterfowl impoundments (moist-soil areas), and waterfowl impoundments (cropland) (Table 1 and Figure 5).

Bottomland Hardwood Forest

Clearing of what is now Grand Cote Refuge began in the late 1960s. The land is now largely cleared except a few remnant tracts of mature bottomland hardwood forests totaling 35 acres. Approximately 1,576 acres have naturally regenerated to bottomland hardwood forest species and refuge staff have reforested 1,186 acres to bottomland hardwood forest species, totaling 2,797 acres overall. Species planted include nuttall oak, water oak, willow oak, bitter pecan, and cypress.

Upland Forest

The refuge currently has 273 acres of upland forest located next to the Headquarters' Office. There has been little to no management of this upland forest and species composition consists of mainly nonnative tree species, including Chinese tallow and long-leaf pine.

Table 1. Summary of existing habitat types at Grand Cote National Wildlife Refuge

Habitat Type	Existing Acreage
Remnant Bottomland Hardwood Forest	35
Natural Regeneration	1,576
Reforestation	1,186
Upland Forest	273
Waterfowl Impoundments - Cropland	1,945
Waterfowl Impoundments - Moist-soil	585
Bayous/Levees/Roads/Parking and Facilities	475
TOTAL	**6,075**

Waterfowl Imoundments

General

Currently, the refuge maintains 20 miles of levees, 25 water control structures, 7 irrigation wells, and 2 low-lift pumps, which provide the infrastructure for all water management activities on the refuge. There are 29 waterfowl impoundments on the refuge, which encompasses 2,530 flooded acres of habitat when completely flooded (Figures 6 and 7). The refuge is divided into two types of waterfowl impoundment management--cropland and moist-soil. Topography of most of the western and central impoundments is generally shallow and flat with water depth during floods ranging from several inches to a maximum of 2 to 3 feet. Variation in topography is greater for impoundments on the eastern end of the refuge, with water depth ranging from several inches to 3-8 feet.

A 1,893-acre block of floodable waterfowl habitat is present in an area north of Little California Road. This area has no water-control structures and few levees. It is dependent on rainfall and/or a rising Coulee Des Grues Bayou for flooding, and generally ebbs and flows with the bayou. Habitats within this area consist of 353 acres of natural regeneration habitat, 1,065 acres of reforested sloughs and bayous, and 475 acres of agricultural land. The placement of water-control structures and some levees in this area has some good potential to create consistent and inexpensive waterfowl habitat within the current waterfowl hunt zone.

Waterfowl Impoundments – Cropland

The refuge currently contains about 1,945 acres of waterfowl impoundments in agricultural crops that are managed to provide wintering waterfowl habitat. To manage the cropland program more efficiently, the refuge is divided into two farm units. This division is along Choctaw Bayou, which divides the refuge into East Farm and West Farm Units (Figures 6 and 7). Within these units, cooperative farmers operate within distinct boundaries. The West Farm Unit is located west of Choctaw Bayou while the East Farm Unit is located east of the bayou.

Figure 5. General habitat types on Grand Cote National Wildlife Refuge

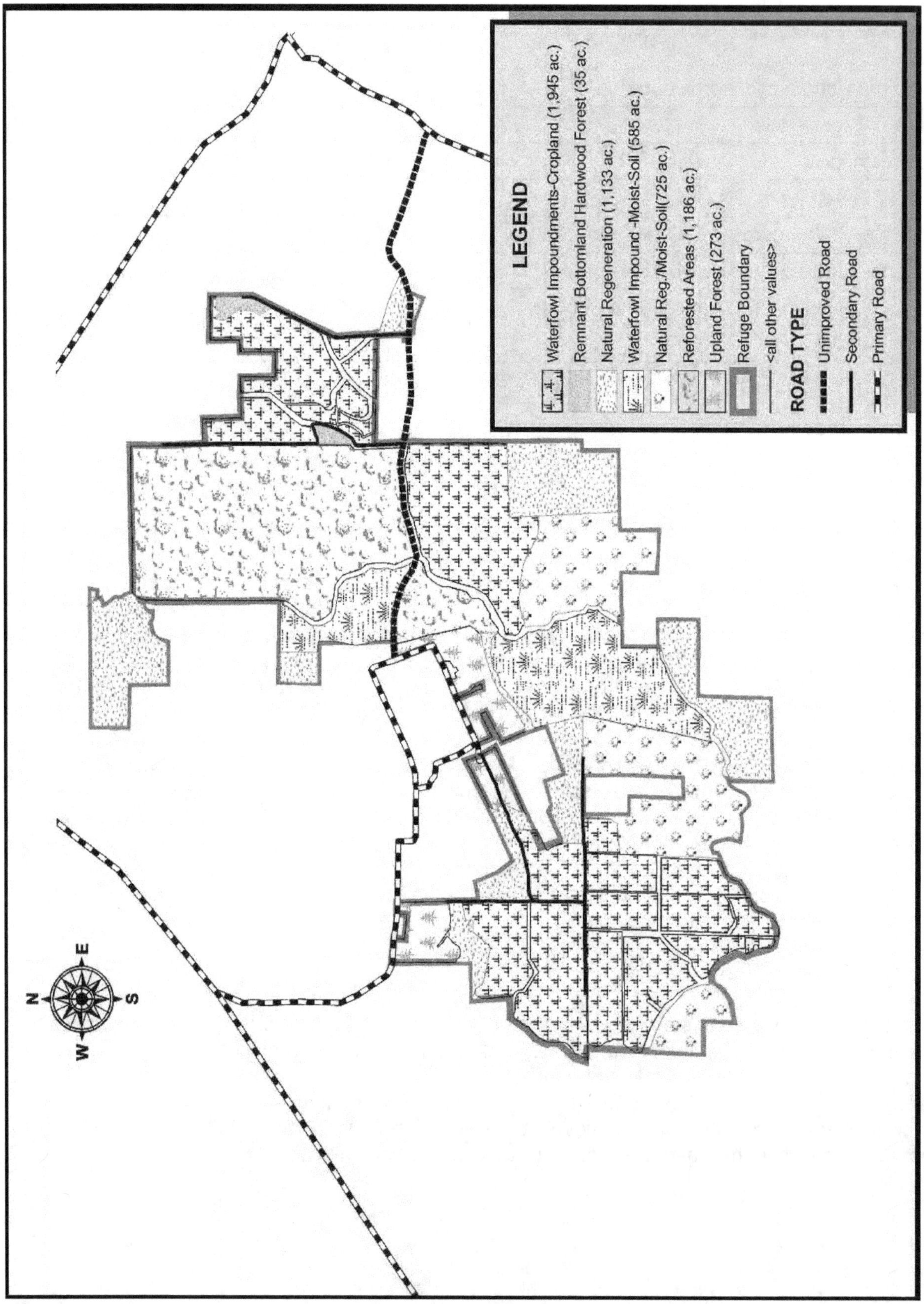

LEGEND

Waterfowl Impoundments-Cropland (1,945 ac.)
Remnant Bottomland Hardwood Forest (35 ac.)
Natural Regeneration (1,133 ac.)
Waterfowl Impound -Moist-Soil (585 ac.)
Natural Reg./Moist-Soil(725 ac.)
Reforested Areas (1,186 ac.)
Upland Forest (273 ac.)
Refuge Boundary
<all other values>

ROAD TYPE

Unimproved Road
Secondary Road
Primary Road

Figure 6. Waterfowl impoundments in the West Farm Unit, Grand Cote National Wildlife Refuge

Figure 7. Waterfowl impoundments in the East Farm Unit, Grand Cote National Wildlife Refuge

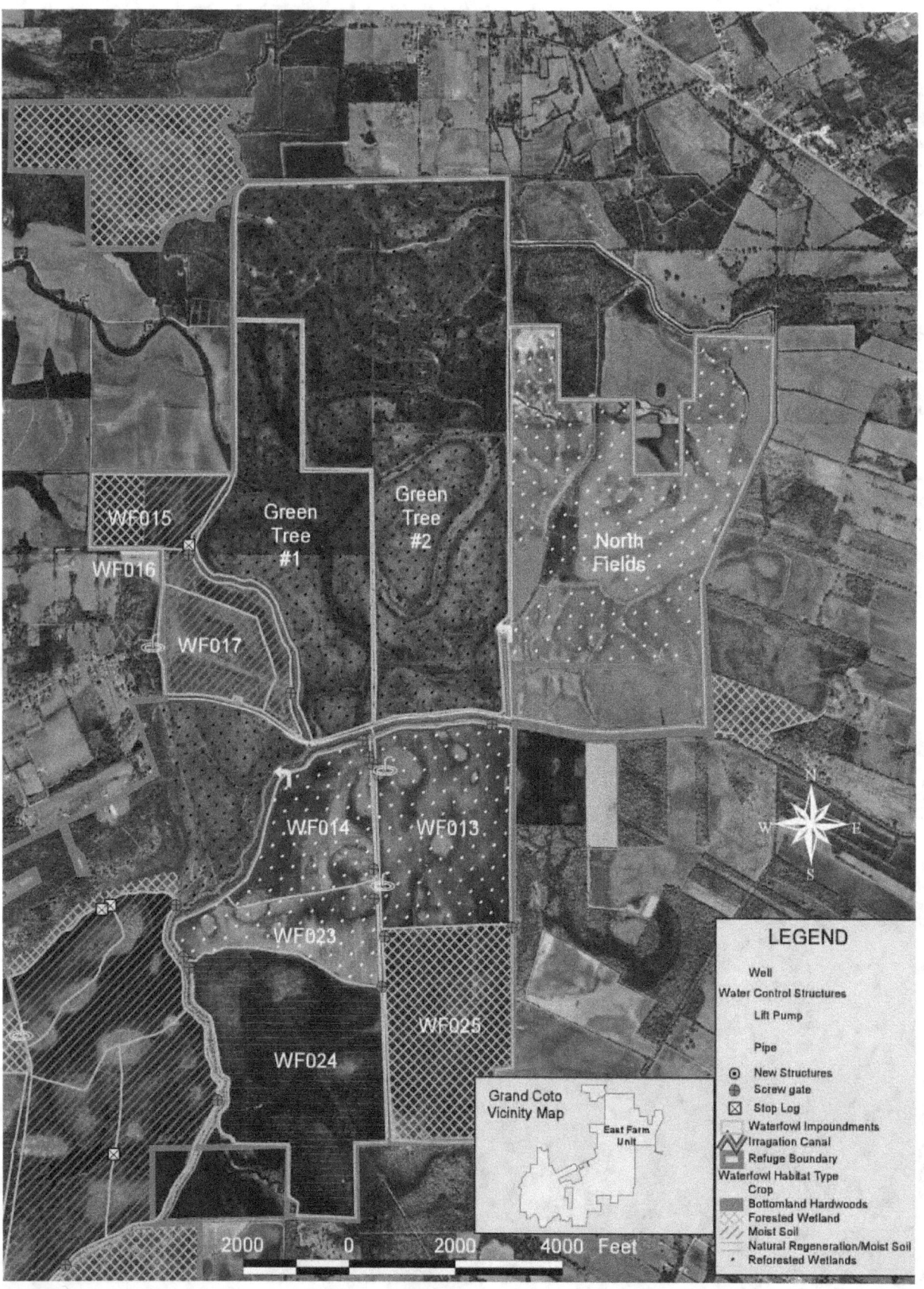

Currently, cooperative farmers perform in-kind services as payment or leave a percent of the crops unharvested in the field for wildlife. Utilizing farmer services achieves two objectives: 1) allows the refuge to maintain moist-soil areas that otherwise would be neglected due to lack of resources, and 2) provide "hot food" for waterfowl in order to help achieve Louisiana step down objectives. More importantly, cooperative farmers' in-kind services 1) help maximize waterbird management overall on non-forested lands; 2) improve water management capabilities; and 3) allow diversification of habitat across the refuge, such as millet, soybeans, rice, milo, sunflower, moist-soil, etc. Operating an effective and productive moist-soil program is very costly, both in terms of dollars and personnel. Utilizing services from farmers provides a unique opportunity to achieve a diverse food base, produce a large quantity of highly nutritious food, and make foods available for a diverse group of organisms. The presence of the farming program also provides critical shallow-water habitat for waterfowl and shorebirds.

West Farm Unit

The West Farm Unit consists of approximately 1,064 acres, and includes milo, soybeans, and rice. These crop types are grown annually and farmers are restricted to planting only waterfowl food. Services in the West Farm Unit have been targeted at improving water management efficiency and increased rice/moist-soil production. Since 1998, about 160 acres have been laser leveled, and deferred maintenance allocations have provided for the drilling of two irrigation wells. Future improvements would continue enhancing rice, moist-soil production, and water management capabilities by leveling more ground, cleaning ditches, and installing underground pipe for more efficient water conveyance.

East Farm Unit

The East Farm Unit consists of approximately 950 acres, and includes milo and soybeans. Currently, there is no rice production in the East Farm Unit. Services in this unit have been targeted at setting back vegetation succession for increasing moist-soil production and planting millet. Approximately 90 acres have been cleaned up and are planted to millet annually. Future improvements include: 1) enhancing rice and moist-soil production, and water management capability south of Little California Road; and 2) establishing water management through delivery and drainage north of Little California Road.

Waterfowl Impoundments - Moist-soil Units

The refuge currently contains about 585 acres of moist-soil waterfowl impoundments that are managed to provide wintering waterfowl habitat (Figures 6 and 7). Moist-soil management propagates natural, wetland plants that produce seeds or tubers high in protein and other nutrients that are a seasonally important component of the diets of migrating and wintering waterfowl. These areas also produce habitats rich in invertebrates, which are an important source of protein for waterfowl during spring and fall migration. Cover created in most moist-soil units are also a crucial habitat component for ducks, particularly during the pair-bonding period.

The timing of drawdowns in waterfowl impoundments on Grand Cote Refuge to propagate moist-soil plants has ranged from mid-March, for annual smartweed production, to late-June to maximize sprangletop and barnyard grass production. Water depth in the surrounding bayou/coulee is another factor that determines the draw down schedules. Most drawdowns are considered slow, at approximately three inches per week.

Some common desirable moist-soil plants found in impoundments on the refuge are annual smartweed, sprangletop, red-rooted sedge, and wild millets (e.g., barnyard grass and jungle rice). Estimated pounds/acre of seeds for these moist-soil plants (Laubhan 1992) have ranged from 252 to 588 pounds per acre (minus red rooted sedge, with red rooted sedge = 403- 19,297 lbs/acre) in moist-soil sites on the refuge during 2002 and 2003. Red vine, alligator weed, coffeeweed, trumpet creeper, cocklebur, button bush, and willow trees are some common nuisance plants found in moist-soil units on the refuge. Disking, flooding, and applying herbicides are common practices used when nuisance plants become a problem. Generally units are disked and planted in millet at least once every three years for nuisance plant control.

Fall flooding for wintering waterfowl, in a typical year, begins around late-November or early-December and is usually rain-dependent. Impoundments are generally flooded at half capacity during this time and gradually the water is raised until full capacity around late-January, making food available to waterfowl as the water rises. The water is generally dropped gradually after this time period to concentrate invertebrates for waterfowl. Pumping early water (in September) in impoundments is generally conducted in a few areas each year for shorebirds and teal, but is not common due to expense.

WILDLIFE

Winter Waterfowl Use

Wintering waterfowl species common on the area includes northern pintail, blue-winged teal, green-winged teal, mallard, gadwall, American wigeon, northern shoveler, and wood duck (migratory and resident). Occasional use by large numbers of divers, such as lesser scaup, ring-necked duck, and redhead, occurs in some of the deeper, more open impoundments on the east end of the refuge.

A breakdown of total duck use by percent for the winter of 2002-03 indicates that "divers" (28 percent) were the largest user group, followed by northern shoveler (20 percent), gadwall (18 percent), mallard (15 percent), and green-winged teal (11 percent). Bimonthly waterfowl surveys for Grand Cote Refuge, for a 5-year period, indicate that duck numbers are generally low in October and November, peak during the months of December or January, and then drop off significantly in February and March. Numbers have ranged from a high of 44,734 ducks during December 2002-03, and zero birds counted during October and November 2000-01 and 2001-02. Limited or no water and mild weather generally limit duck numbers during these months. A refuge record high of 1 million duck-use-days plus were recorded on 18 different waterfowl impoundments on Grand Cote Refuge during the winter of 2001-02. The majority of these duck-use-days occurred from December to February.

Goose use of harvested agricultural fields on the refuge has been as high as 16,000 birds, but is usually short term. The most numerous goose species present are snow geese, white-fronted geese, and Canada geese, respectively.

Resident Waterfowl Use

Resident wood ducks are common on the refuge with breeding/production limited by the lack of natural and artificial cavities and quality brood habitat. The current refuge goal is to maintain approximately 75 wood duck boxes. As staff and resources are available, the refuge captures, bands, and releases wood ducks, participating in the Mississippi Flyway Preseason Banding Quotas.

Landbirds

Many species of songbirds are experiencing long-term declines as a result of widespread habitat loss, particularly, bottomland hardwood forests, riparian woodlands, and early successional habitats, such as grasslands and scrub habitats. While the refuge has only 35 acres of mature bottomland hardwood forests, there are more than 1,000 acres of reforested habitat (currently scrub habitat) that will grow into a mature bottomland forest. A large variety of neotropical migratory birds are common in the refuge's different habitat types. Some common year-round residents include the Carolina chickadee, tufted titmouse, northern mocking bird, and red-winged blackbird. Yellow-bellied sapsuckers, white-eyed vireo, hermit thrush, yellow-rumped warbler, and white-throated sparrow are some birds common in the winter.

Raptors frequent the fallow fields and reforested areas in search of rodents. Northern harrier, American kestrel, red-tailed hawk, and Cooper's hawk are some of the raptors observed on this refuge.

Woodcock are showing significant long-term declines in the central and eastern United States. Habitat loss, including the loss of nocturnal wintering habitat, is likely a factor. Although mature bottomland hardwoods are lacking on the refuge, birds may use natural regeneration and agricultural fields as nighttime foraging habitat. The abundance of woodcock on the refuge has not been quantified to date, but they should be present in suitable habitat.

Mourning doves are common on the refuge and are generally found feeding in harvested agricultural fields or roosting in reforested and fallow field habitats. Abundance of these birds is dependent on weather, distribution, and amount of food, water, and roosting sites on the refuge and surrounding property.

Shorebirds

Shorebirds migrate through the Mississippi Alluvial Valley from the southernmost part of South America to the northernmost part of North America. They typically probe in soft mud (e.g., mudflats) and shallow water for worms and small crustaceans. In the Mississippi Alluvial Valley, these birds generally migrate through during spring and fall, foraging as they migrate. They may only spend 10 days in the valley. Few shorebirds overwinter or nest in the valley. Habitat is generally more limited during their fall migration than in the spring. Quality shorebird habitat is also limited on the refuge during this time primarily due to the best shallow-water sites being in some form of agriculture. Shorebirds observed on the refuge during 2001-2003 were killdeer, willets, least sandpipers, lesser yellowlegs, black-necked stilts, pectoral sandpipers, solitary sandpipers, and common snipes. Black-necked stilts have nested on the refuge. The refuge also annually provides 50 acres of shallow-water habitat in August and September.

Wading and Marsh Birds

Wading birds are abundant in the refuge's waterfowl impoundments, canals, and bayous throughout the year. Species regularly observed include green herons, cattle egrets, snowy egrets, great egrets, little blue herons, great blue herons, yellow and black-crowned night herons, anhingas, white ibis, glossy ibis, wood storks, and tricolor herons. No wading bird rookeries have been located on the refuge within the last 5 years.

Several sandhill crane roost sites are located west of the refuge on private land, with one of the larger roosts being located on the Chatlin Lake acquisition site. Cranes begin appearing in small numbers in early-November, gradually build until their numbers peak in late-February, and by mid-March they all have completely migrated north. Peak numbers have ranged from approximately 900 to 1,500 from 2002-2004. Local landowners recall first observing a few birds (25-40) during the late 1970s, with their numbers gradually building every year. After leaving the roost, sandhill cranes can be found foraging in harvested rice, corn, or sugar cane fields many miles away from their roost sites.

King rail, least bittern, pied-billed grebe, American coot, and purple gallinule are all species in decline locally and/or regionally due to the loss of freshwater emergent wetlands. It is possible that all of these wading birds occur at Grand Cote Refuge.

Threatened and Endangered Species

Although no bald eagles have been reported on the refuge in recent history, the potential for wintering birds is possible due to the large concentrations of waterfowl that occur on the refuge. Black bear habitat on the refuge is very limited and the possibility of a dispersing or wandering Louisiana black bear visiting the refuge is remote, but possible. Eleven adult female Louisiana black bears and 26 cubs were released on Lake Ophelia Refuge (approximately 30 miles to the north) during the spring of 2003 and 2004, as part of the Louisiana black bear repatriation project.

Species of Concern

Ospreys, wood storks, northern harriers, swallow-tail kites, and alligator snapping turtles are all species of special concern occasionally reported in this area. Late season drawdowns of waterfowl impoundments often attract post-breeding wood storks to the refuge.

Mammals

White-tailed deer appear to be abundant based on general observations. Limited deer population surveys have been conducted to date; however, general observations and available habitat all point to a healthy and abundant deer herd. A 3-month either-sex deer archery hunt was conducted for the first time in 2003. The harvest objective is to maintain as close as possible a one-to-one buck/doe ratio. The target harvest, per-square-mile, is a conservative 1 deer per 100 acres. This will be the refuge's objective until population surveys (e.g., spotlight, cameras, or browse survey) are conducted or harvest data is analyzed to obtain baseline information on the deer herd that will justify a change. The refuge consists of a mixture of farm fields, reforestation, moist-soil impoundments, and bottomland hardwood forests, which create a mosaic of different habitats that provide excellent cover and forage for deer and other wildlife.

Swamp rabbits and cottontail rabbits appear to be abundant on the refuge. Natural regeneration habitat, reforested areas, and agricultural fields are intermingled and provide plenty of food and cover in close proximity for these two species. Fox and gray squirrel numbers are limited due to the lack of mature bottomland hardwood forests (35 acres).

A number of furbearers, including nutria, raccoon, mink, opossum, coyote, bobcat, beaver, river otter, and striped-skunk, are thought to be abundant on the refuge. Beaver, muskrat, river otter, nutria, and mink are associated with the more permanently inundated wetlands and bayous. The raccoon is well adapted to all existing habitats, and the opossum, coyote, and bobcat are mostly associated with drier forests and brushy fields. Little or no formal data are available to provide population estimates for these species. However, general observations indicate that the number of beaver and raccoons has increased in recent years, likely due to a decrease in fur prices. These two species are of concern because of their potential to significantly impact ecosystems.

Nuisance Wildlife

Some unregulated nuisance animals on the refuge include coyote, feral hog, raccoon, nutria, and beaver. These species are thought to occur throughout the refuge in varying densities. Several species, including hog and beaver, may destroy or change the habitat, or in the case of feral hogs, compete with native wildlife for limited food resources and thus have a negative impact on other wildlife species (e.g., deer, squirrels, and songbirds). Beavers manipulate hydrology both on and off the refuge by constructing dams that inundate bottomland hardwood forests for prolonged periods. Predation of nests and females by raccoons may adversely affect populations of breeding neotropical migratory birds, wood ducks, turkeys, or wading birds.

Reptiles and Amphibians

Amphibian management and conservation are of great interest due to apparent global amphibian declines. Habitat loss, fragmentation, and degradation appear to be the primary factors in declines. This group of animals requires quality wetland habitat for its survival and it serves as an important indicator of overall environmental health. Although no amphibian and reptile surveys have been conducted on the refuge to determine species occurrence or population levels, a species list was developed for the refuge based on surveys in similar habitats (Appendix VII).

Fisheries

Permanent water is the main factor that limits the fisheries resource on Grand Cote Refuge, with Choctaw Bayou and Coulee Des Grues being its only permanent water. Fish species that occur in these bayous are freshwater drum, bigmouth and small mouth buffalo, channel catfish, shortnose and spotted gar, bowfin, largemouth bass, black crappie and bluegill. Numerous species of mussels are also thought to occur within these bayous. A limited amount of spawning by fish trapped by backwater flooding occurs within flooded impoundments in early spring before drawdowns occur, with fry being released into the bayous during drawdowns.

Crawfish is an important fisheries resource on the refuge with many thousands of pounds being harvested from April through May by recreational fishermen. Although abundance of crawfish has not been quantified, their numbers appear to be dependent on impoundment management activities, such as timing of fall flood and spring drawdowns. Numbers are generally higher after several wet years and lower after several dry years. Wading birds, raccoons, and mink are a few of the species that are seasonally dependent on crawfish for food.

Surveys

Currently, shorebird, waterfowl and wading birds, and sandhill crane surveys are being conducted on the refuge. Shorebird surveys are conducted annually during August and September to determine yearly trends in species, numbers, and habitat. Data are forwarded to the Lower Mississippi Valley Joint Venture for compiling and analysis. Waterfowl/wading birds are surveyed bimonthly (ground) on predetermined dates (set to be conducted concurrently across the Region) from October to mid-March. Species, numbers, and water gauge levels are recorded for each impoundment and compiled to determine trends and general habitat use. An aerial, mid-winter waterfowl survey is conducted annually for Grand Cote Refuge and surrounding private lands. Weekly sandhill crane roost surveys are conducted from the time of their arrival in November to their departure by early March to determine population trends and migration patterns. All survey data are entered into a GIS or ACCESS database.

Monitoring

Moist-soil management activities are monitored, recorded, and entered into a database as general recordkeeping and as a means to determine plant responses from management activities for optimal production. Some parameters that are monitored and recorded are drawdown schedules, soil moisture, plant species present, percent coverage, and seed production estimations. The refuge staff will continue to monitor duck use and maintain wood duck nest boxes.

Trapping and Banding

The refuge annually traps and bands wood ducks to help meet flyway and state banding goals.

Research

A limited amount of research has been conducted on the refuge. Currently, Grand Cote Refuge is one of 67 sites being monitored by David G. Krementz and Robert H. Doster from the Arkansas Cooperative Fish and Wildlife Research Unit, as part of a study to determine the importance of Mississippi Alluvial Valley reforestation and wetland restoration sites to wintering birds.

CULTURAL RESOURCES

The refuge has not been subjected to systematic archaeological and historic investigations. However, a number of archaeological investigations has occurred in the vicinity; the majority being conducted by the Works Progress Administration in association with Louisiana State University between 1938 through 1941. The early excavations focused upon the large multiple mound sites, such as the Marksville and the Greenhouse Sites, and were pivotal in elucidating the Marksville and the Troyville-Coles Creek Cultures (Neuman 1984). Neitzel identified a large post-1780 historic Tunica-Biloxi village in his 1939 survey of the parish. This site is part of the Tunica-Biloxi Reservation. Toth (1974) synthesized the WPA-LSU excavations at the Marksville Site, basing his refinement of Marksville Phase on ceramic analysis. Jones and Shuman (1989 and 1990) verified the locations of 37 mound sites scattered across Avoyelles Parish, documented their current status, and created base maps.

The landscape has been heavily influenced by evolution of the Red and Mississippi Rivers over the past 300,000 years (Jones and Shuman 1989; Saucier 1994). Jones and Shuman (1989) noted that the Rivers' floodplains, which cover about 750 of the parish's 850 square miles, contain lakes, old stream beds, natural levees, and crevasses in the levees. The Pleistocene-era Prairie Terraces span eastern Rapides and western Avoyelles Parishes. The Avoyelles Prairie Terrace represents the first upland area on the Red River above the Red-Mississippi Rivers' confluence that is not subject to periodic inundation. A number of older and modern stream courses, like Bayou Des Grues, Choctaw Bayou, and Bayou Rouge, flow through the land form. Many of these occupy former channels of the Red or Mississippi Rivers. The Prairie Terrace, as well as the natural levees of the stream courses, provided living surfaces for pre-columbian and historic occupations. The refuge is described as a giant natural sump south and west of the Red River. The bottomland hardwood forest that covered this area was cleared for agricultural purposes in the 1970s. To facilitate drainage, a system of levees was subsequently constructed. The archaeological potential, which was low due to the topography, the hydrological regime, and the presence of poorly drained clayey soils, was further reduced.

SOCIOECONOMIC ENVIRONMENT

Grand Cote Refuge lies in the west central portion of Avoyelles Parish. Avoyelles Parish is near the center of Louisiana and is bounded by Rapides Parish on the west; LaSalle and Catahoula Parishes on the north; Concordia Parish on the northwest; Pointe Coupee Parish to the southeast; St. Landry Parish to the south; and Evangeline Parish to the southwest. The Old River and Atchafalaya River form the southeastern boundary of Avoyelles Parish. The Red River flows through the northern portion of the parish.

Traditionally, Avoyelles Parish has not been in the forefront of economic growth or development in the State of Louisiana, and historically, unemployment figures in the double digits have been common. Instead, much of the economic and social life of the area centers on neighboring Rapides Parish and the city of Alexandria.

Avoyelles Parish is predominantly rural, with the largest town and parish seat being Marksville (6,087). As in other rural areas throughout the country, outdoor activities are both popular and necessary. Hunting and recreational fishing are popular pastimes, and farming, commercial fishing, and forestry are important elements of the economy.

EARLY SETTLEMENT OF AVOYELLES PARISH

Avoyelles Parish received its name from the tribe of Avoyelles Indians that resided there when the first European settlers arrived. Native Americans play an important role in Avoyelles Parish, as the Tunica-Biloxi Indians are the largest employer, employing 1,100 employees out of an estimated labor force of 15,860 in 1997 (Louisiana Department of Economic Development 1998).

The first European settlers in Avoyelles Parish were the French. In Avoyelles Parish, the prairie land was settled first. The early settlers were primarily self-sufficient. Game and fish were plentiful. Cattle and pigs were allowed to roam the woods freely, and along with poultry, could be raised at little expense. Corn, rice, and fruit were grown for personal consumption, while indigo was the primary cash crop, with some tobacco cultivation.

Around 1780, the area became known as Avoyelles Post. The post became an important center for trade, first between European settlers and Indians, then later as a merchandising center for the area (Avoyelles Parish Planning Board 1947). Later settlers settled along the streams, where the land was very fertile and the streams could serve as sources of transportation. Canoes and flatboats were used to carry merchandise and were the primary methods of transportation.

In the early 1800s, cotton began to replace indigo as the main money crop, and in 1804 a cotton gin was built in Avoyelles Parish (Saucier 1943). The cotton farms were primarily small farms in the highlands. Although these higher lands were safe from floods, transporting the cotton to the river landings was sometimes a problem.

In 1815, the first steamboat went up the Red River, and by 1875, when navigation on the river began to decline, there were 52 boats traveling the Red River (Saucier 1943). The Old River, the Bayou des Glaises, Lake Long, and Bayou Rouge were other navigable streams that were also used to transport cotton bales.

LAND USE

Avoyelles Parish is predominantly rural. In 1990, 66.4 percent of the population lived in rural areas, with 6 percent living on farms (U.S. Department of Commerce, Bureau of the Census 1990). In 1992, 48 percent of the total land area was utilized by farms (U.S. Department of Commerce, Bureau of the Census 1996). There were 953 farms, with an average size of 269 acres. This was slightly smaller than the average size of a farm in Louisiana, which was 306 acres (U.S. Department of Commerce, Bureau of the Census 1992).

The number of farms, along with the total acreage in farmland, has declined over the past 10 years. At the same time, the average size of a farm has increased, mirroring a trend that is occurring across the nation.

DEMOGRAPHICS

Avoyelles Parish is primarily rural, with a total estimated population of 41,981 in 2004 (Louisiana Department of Economic Development 2004). The parish actually lost population between 1980 and 1990. The 1980 population of Avoyelles Parish was 41,393, but by 1990 the population had declined to 38,159 (U.S. Department of Commerce 1980, 1990). Marksville, the parish seat, is the largest town.

In 2000, the majority of the population was Caucasian, 29 percent were African-American, 1.0 percent was Hispanic; and 1.0 percent was Native American. In 2000, the median family income was $23,851, with 24 percent of the population falling below the poverty level (Louisiana Department of Economic Development 2000).

EMPLOYMENT

The service industry is the largest employer in Avoyelles Parish, employing 46.7 percent of employees, due in large part to the Paragon Casino (the largest single employer), which employs more than 1,000 employees (Louisiana Department of Economic Development 1998).

Employment in the parish in other economic sectors generally has been stable. The sectors employing the largest numbers of persons were in decreasing order as follows: the service industry, retail trade, public administration, manufacturing, construction, finance, transportation, and agriculture (Louisiana Department of Economic Development 2000).

RECREATION

Avoyelles Parish has always had an abundance of fish and game, due to its diversity of lands and waters. As early as 1939, a sportsmen's club was created for the purpose of protecting game and wildlife (Saucier 1943).

Refuge Recreational Use. Grand Cote Refuge contains moderate populations of fish and wildlife, including a number of game species. Indeed, these provide the primary recreational activities occurring on the refuge, namely public hunting and fishing. Hunting and fishing are provided in accordance with federal, state, and refuge regulations.

Crawfishing is the most popular activity on the refuge, with 1,000-2,000 participants during 2004. The refuge opened to hunting for the first time during the fall hunting season of 2003, with 1,000 participants. Deer (archery only) and waterfowl may be taken on the refuge during the appropriate seasons. Beaver, feral hogs, nutria, raccoon, and coyote may be taken during game seasons. Large portions of the refuge are accessible for hunting only by all-terrain vehicle trails, which are open only during the hunting season.

Outdoor Recreation Economics. In addition to those on the refuge, the fish and game of Avoyelles Parish are economically important in two ways. First, a considerable commercial fishery is present in both the Red and Atchafalaya Rivers, along with local aquaculture operations. Crawfish and catfish are the major species harvested, and the buffalo fish is also important. Second, hunting and fishing are economically important to local businesses, both directly, as the local population spends money, and indirectly, as an attraction that draws sportsmen from outside the parish.

Unfortunately, a general lack of regard for the conservation of fish and wildlife resources combined with wetland clearing and draining, has led to the loss of valuable fishery spawning grounds and to the loss of habitat for many wildlife species. In an attempt to restore and protect some of these resources, the refuge serves an important role of providing habitat for plant and wildlife species and a place where people can go to enjoy these resources, either through observation or, more directly, through hunting or fishing.

When improved access, facilities, and staffing are added, the refuge can serve as an important commodity in the economic life of the community. Ecotourism, hunting, fishing, wildlife observation, wildlife photography, and environmental interpretation are increasingly being seen as a desirable industry. As the population increases and the number of places left to enjoy wildlife decreases, the refuge may become even more important to the local community. It can benefit the community directly by providing recreational opportunities for the local population, and indirectly by attracting tourists from outside the parish to generate additional dollars to the local economy.

TRANSPORTATION

In its early days, Avoyelles Parish relied on water transportation. The rivers and bayous that crisscross the parish served as a means for transportation, trade, and communication for almost every community within the parish (Avoyelles Parish Planning Board 1947). Some of the important waterways within the parish were the Red, Old, and Atchafalaya Rivers, and the Rouge, Des Glaises, Choctaw, and Boef Bayous. While today these waterways are no longer necessary for most of the transportation needs within the parish, they are still important as sources of income and for recreation.

Interstate Highway 49 and U.S. Highway 71 run through the southwestern portion of the parish, while Louisiana State Highway 1 runs through the center. A number of smaller roads connect the various communities within the parish.

Grand Cote Refuge is in the west central part of Avoyelles Parish and can be reached via Louisiana Highway 1194, a mostly paved road from Highway 1. All roads within the refuge are unpaved and are unsuitable for some vehicles. This is one of the primary factors limiting recreational use on the refuge.

VISITOR SERVICES

The National Wildlife Refuge System Improvement Act of 1997 allows six priority public uses on national wildlife refuges as long as they are compatible with the purposes for which the refuge was established. These include hunting, fishing, wildlife observation, wildlife photography, and

---

environmental education and interpretation. With the establishment of a hunting program, the refuge now provides hunting, fishing, and limited wildlife observation (Figure 8).

HUNTING

Grand Cote Refuge is strategically located in central Louisiana and is influenced by both the Mississippi and Central Flyways. Catahoula Lake (30 miles north) and Lacassine and Sabine National Wildlife Refuges (120 miles south) have historically held a large number of wintering waterfowl, especially northern pintails. Grand Cote Refuge is positioned between Catahoula Lake and the coastal refuges and provides an important sanctuary area between these two historic wintering areas. Due to the strategic location, the refuge was established to provide critical habitat for migratory waterfowl. Currently, approximately 3,675 acres are maintained as sanctuary where all public entry is prohibited from November 1 to February 28 each year.

The refuge opened to hunting for the first time during the fall hunting season of 2003. The refuge was opened for waterfowl, deer, mourning dove, woodcock, and rabbit hunting. Also, beaver, feral hogs, nutria, raccoon, and coyote may be taken incidental to any refuge hunt with weapons legal for that hunt. Hunting is permitted in designated areas only. Retrieving dogs are permitted for waterfowl hunts and rabbit dogs are permitted after the close of the Louisiana deer gun season. The refuge requires an annual hunting permit for all hunters 16 years of age or older. A youth waterfowl hunt is offered under a lottery system. There are three blinds available for this hunt. The refuge participates in the state Youth Waterfowl Weekend. Special arrangements can be made to accommodate persons with bona fide disabilities. The refuge also offers space blind waterfowl lottery hunts. Hunters under the age of 16 must possess proof of completion of an approved Hunter Safety Course and be accompanied at all times by an adult 21 years of age or older. Archery hunters (regardless of age) must possess proof of completion of the International Bow Hunter Education Course. Refuge staff participates in the annual Louisiana State Hunt Coordination meeting hosted by the Louisiana Department of Wildlife and Fisheries.

FISHING

Sport fishing is permitted year-round in the Coulee Des Grues along Little California Road. Anglers may harvest any fish species on the refuge that is permitted by state regulations. State fish size and bag limits apply. Creel limits, boating safety, and license requirements are in accordance with state regulations unless otherwise specified in the fishing brochure. Recreational crawfishing is permitted in designated areas of the refuge with pyramid nets from April 1 through May 31. The harvest is limited to 100 pounds per permit holder per day. No commercial crawfishing is permitted. All crawfishing gear, including nets, boats, bait, and trash, must be removed from refuge property after each visit. Crawfishing has been the primary public use on the refuge with approximately 1,000 – 2,000 people utilizing the refuge annually.

NON-CONSUMPTIVE USES

Grand Cote Refuge has one hiking trail, as well as designated levees accessible for hiking during certain times of the year. This trail and levees provide the public an opportunity for wildlife observation and wildlife photography.

Figure 8. Current visitor facilities on Grand Cote National Wildlife Refuge

REFUGE ADMINISTRATION

Grand Cote Refuge is administered from an office located at Central Louisiana National Wildlife Refuge Complex headquarters. This office is responsible for managing the Grand Cote, Lake Ophelia, and Cat Island Refuges, three Farm Service Agency fee title tracts covering a total of 1,990 acres (one each in Avoyelles, Rapides, and St. Landry Parishes), and 13 Farm Service Agency conservation easements (190 and 74 total acres in Avoyelles and Rapides Parishes, respectively) (Figure 2). Although seven staff members report for duty at Grand Cote Refuge and two at Lake Ophelia Refuge, the work responsibilities for each member include duties at all three complex refuges and Farm Service Agency tracts. The complex's current staff includes a Project Leader (GS-0485-13), a Deputy Project Leader (GS-0485-11/12), an Office Assistant (GS-0303-08), a Park Ranger (GS-0025-09), a Wildlife Biologist (GS-0486-11), a Natural Resource Planner (GS-0404-12), a Maintenance Worker (WG-7/8), and two Engineering Equipment Operators (WG-5716-10).

III. Plan Development

PUBLIC INVOLVEMENT AND THE PLANNING PROCESS

In accordance with Service guidelines and National Environmental Policy Act recommendations, public involvement has been a crucial factor throughout the development of this Comprehensive Conservation Plan for Grand Cote National Wildlife Refuge. This plan has been written with input and assistance from interested citizens, conservation organizations, and employees of local and state agencies. The participation of these stakeholders and their ideas has been of great value in setting the management direction for Grand Cote Refuge. The Service, as a whole, and the refuge staff, in particular, are very grateful to each one who has contributed time, expertise, and ideas to the planning process. The staff remains impressed by the passion and commitment of so many individuals for the lands and waters administered by the refuge.

A planning team (Appendix VIII) was formed to prepare the both the draft plan and environmental assessment and the final plan. Initially, the team focused on identifying the issues and concerns pertinent to refuge management. The team met on several occasions from February 2004 to April 2006.

In preparation for developing the Draft Plan and Environmental Assessment, a Biological Review was conducted during the week of October 20-22, 2003, by a team of Service biologists, managers, foresters, and non-service managers/biologists (see Chapter V). The Biological Review was completed in February 2004. A Visitor Services Review was completed in November 2003. To expand the range of issues and generate potential alternatives, public input to the development of the Draft Plan was initiated through two public scoping meetings held on March 9 and 11, 2004, at Marksville and Bunkie High Schools, Avoyelles Parish, Louisiana. At the meetings, interested stakeholders were able to register their concerns to ensure that they would be considered in the development of the Draft Plan. The meeting dates were publicized in local papers in the cities of Alexandria, Marksville, Ville Platte, Jena, Bunkie, and Lafayette, Louisiana, and were broadcasted on two local radio stations. There were 19 attendees at the meetings, and several meeting attendees provided public comment. One citizen sent a comment letter to the refuge.

The issues and alternatives generated from these meetings, coupled with the input of the planning team, are summarized below. A draft plan was developed for the refuge, which, when approved by the Fish and Wildlife Service, will direct management of the refuge over a 15-year period.

SUMMARY OF ISSUES, CONCERNS, AND OPPORTUNITIES

The planning team identified a number of issues, concerns, and opportunities related to fish and wildlife populations, habitat restoration and management, hunting, fishing, and community outreach and education. Additionally, the planning team considered federal and state mandates, as well as applicable local ordinances, regulations, and plans. The team also directed the process of obtaining public input through public scoping meetings, comment packets, and personal comments. All public and advisory team comments were considered; however, some issues important to the public fall outside the scope of the decision to be made within this planning process. The team considered all issues raised throughout this planning process, and has developed a plan that attempts to balance the competing opinions regarding important issues. The team identified those issues that, in the team's best professional judgment, are most significant to the refuge. A detailed summary of the significant issues follows.

FISH AND WILDLIFE POPULATION MANAGEMENT

Waterfowl

The refuge's waterfowl purpose guides most operation and management actions. A portion of the refuge is dedicated to providing seasonally flooded croplands, moist soil, and forested wetlands to meet the feeding, resting, and breeding needs of migratory and resident waterfowl. A 2003 Biological Review of the refuge identified objectives needed to provide sufficient water, food, sanctuary, resting/loafing, and wintering areas to meet the habitat and population goals of the North American Waterfowl Management Plan, as stepped down through the Lower Mississippi Valley Joint Venture (Table 2).

Table 2. Louisiana step-down and Mississippi Flyway objectives

Current Waterfowl and Habitat Objectives*				
Moist Soil	Bottomland Hardwoods	Unharvested Cropland	Harvested Crop	Duck Use Days
900 acres	500 acres	200 acres	500 acres	7,548,700

* Waterfowl and habitat objectives are being revised as part of an NAWMP update.

The Review Team concluded that additional waterfowl habitat would need to be protected and managed in non-sanctuary areas of the refuge to support wintering waterfowl and provide public waterfowl hunting opportunities.

Improving the wood duck nest box program was also identified in the public scoping process. The refuge is looking to expand and improve the wood duck nest box program and increase quality brood habitat for breeding waterfowl.

Surveys and Monitoring

Currently, few surveys and monitoring programs are implemented on the refuge. Moist-soil productivity monitoring, winter waterfowl counts, wood duck box monitoring, and shorebird surveys are conducted annually. A limited number of deer spotlighting surveys has been conducted.

Inventorying bobcats to determine which subspecies occurs on the refuge, testing turtles for methyl-mercury levels to determine if consumption notices should be posted, working with the Service's Ecological Services Field Office to list alligator snapping turtles, and studying the potential to release hatchling alligator snapping turtles on the refuge are all wishes identified during the public scoping process. The refuge is proposing to expand its monitoring and surveying programs to include resident wildlife, fish, amphibians, reptiles, and many other species.

Invasive Plants and Animals

Currently, the refuge does not have a concise inventory and quantitative analysis of the invasive plants and animals that occur. Increasing coyote harvest and not opening a bobcat season on the refuge were wishes identified during the public scoping process. The refuge plans on inventorying and monitoring invasive plant and animal species and developing a management plan to best address these concerns.

Bottomland Hardwood Forest

The refuge currently consists of 1,576 acres of naturally regenerated bottomland hardwoods, 1,186 acres of reforested bottomland hardwoods, 35 acres of remnant bottomland hardwood forest, and 273 acres of upland forest.

Reforesting the entire refuge, to reforesting only the bottom areas in crop fields, to reforesting areas north of Little California Road were suggestions identified during the public scoping process. The idea of providing a diversity of habitats on the refuge and not reforesting the entire area was also expressed. Also, management practices of bottomland hardwood forests, especially those adjacent to inholdings, are a concern to some adjoining landowners.

The refuge is not included in the Partners in Flight Bird Conservation Plan to support key populations of neotropical migratory birds. Large blocks of contiguous forest (i.e., core forest area at least 1 kilometer [0.62 mile] from forest edge] are needed to support healthy populations of neotropical migratory birds. The area surrounding the refuge has been mostly cleared for agriculture. The small amount of bottomland hardwood forest that exists in and around the refuge is not large enough to support source populations of neotropical migratory birds and instead could potentially act as an ecological trap or habitat sink. The Biological Review Team determined that even if completely reforested, the refuge would not meet minimum criteria to support most priority forest-associated bird species.

Waterfowl Impoundment Management

A common agricultural practice in rice culture operations is a process of mechanically precision leveling farm fields to maximize water efficiency and thereby rice production. The primary purpose of this practice, as promoted by the Natural Resources Conservation Service and the Louisiana State University Agricultural Extension Service, is to conserve groundwater and reduce the pumping cost by at least 10-15 percent over fairly flat fields, facilitate management of water depths resulting in more uniform performance and maturation of the crop, and reduce the cost of pulling fewer linear feet of interior levees in cropped fields.

At Grand Cote Refuge, the concept of precision leveling agricultural fields for rice and waterfowl was first established in a 1998 Biological Review. At that time, the refuge did not have the ability to grow rice and precision leveling agricultural ground was a means to promote a rice culture highly attractive to waterfowl, the purpose of the refuge. The refuge was historically bottomland hardwoods until it was cleared in the late 1960s and early 1970s. The lowland/sump nature of the refuge, particularly 1,000 of the remaining 2,000 acres of farmland, is generally flat and conducive to this common agricultural practice.

The 2003 Biological Review recommended that approximately 480 acres be considered for precision leveling; however, lack of leveling may preclude management of some units. On a 6,000-acre refuge, this represents less than 8 percent of the current land base of the refuge and will produce a potential of 3.6 million duck-use-days of foraging habitat or more than 40 percent of the potential duck-use-days of waterfowl foraging habitat provided on the refuge. This will produce nearly one-half the duck-use-day objectives set by the Lower Mississippi Valley Joint Venture.

The process of precision leveling fields moves soil and may result in a field that is less diverse and supports fewer wildlife species than a field of varying topography. The loss of such dynamics may reduce overall productivity; however, diversity among precision-leveled fields may offset individual unit diversity concerns. Because questions remain unanswered, the Biological Review recommended that monitoring and/or research should be conducted to document the overall productivity and wildlife use of precision-leveled versus non-leveled fields.

The Biological Review also recommended exploring the option of force-account farming, which would rely on refuge staff to conduct farming operations for waterfowl. Currently, most of the farming on the refuge is done cooperatively with individuals from the community.

RESOURCE PROTECTION

Land Protection

There are several parcels of land that lie within the existing refuge boundary that are not owned by the Service. Several of these compromise management due to conflicting management purposes and disturbance to wildlife. Acquisition/exchange of these parcels would eliminate access issues, improve management options, and tighten some unclear and confusing boundary issues.

As a result of the Biological Review, it is evident that Grand Cote Refuge is not meeting its waterfowl objectives. In order to account for periodic rehabilitation of wetland units, changes in personnel, and management strategies, it is only realistic to assume the existing fee ownership could provide 80 percent of refuge objectives. As such, the existing fee lands could not, under optimal conditions, meet objectives; therefore, a renewed emphasis should be placed on the Chatlain Lake acquisition area, with land purchases in large enough blocks to realistically and practically make management of the units possible.

Cultural Resources

Archaeological investigations within the refuge have been limited and with the exception of Gibson (1989), have occurred prior to its establishment. The Tunica-Biloxi Native American tribe is located in the local community (tribal lands and Paragon Casino). The Tunica-Biloxi tribe is a strong supporter of natural resource issues and could be a valuable partner.

VISITOR SERVICES

Visitor Services and Education

Currently, little public use occurs besides hunting and fishing. The complex does not have the staff or facilities to provide on- or off-refuge environmental education, interpretive, or non-consumptive wildlife-dependent recreational programs. A boardwalk and observation tower constructed in 2006 provides the public wildlife observation and photography opportunities.

The refuge is in Avoyelles Parish (population 41,860), within 15 miles of the city of Marksville, Louisiana (population 6,087). The Tunica-Biloxi Paragon Casino is a major tourist attraction in the parish, attracting more than 200,000 overnight visitors annually. Many of the casino's overnight hotel and recreational vehicle resort guests are interested in half-day tourist destinations. Visitor facilities in association with a refuge visitor center annex could provide wildlife-dependent environmental education, interpretation, and recreation opportunities currently not available in Avoyelles Parish.

Hunting

Hunting and fishing are integral parts of Louisiana culture. It is not surprising that there is a considerable state and local interest in expanding hunting opportunities. Any additional hunting opportunities will be dependent on providing safe, quality experiences that are compatible with refuge purposes.

Expanding waterfowl hunting opportunities, developing better water control to help facilitate quality hunting and distribution of waterfowl, and decreasing the sanctuary areas are wishes identified during the scoping process. Additional waterfowl hunting opportunities can be provided as the refuge improves water delivery systems and acquires additional land, but the core waterfowl sanctuary needs to remain intact to meet the undisturbed resting and feeding needs of waterfowl. Expanding deer hunting opportunities on the south side of the refuge and having a buck-only archery season were expressed by the public.

Fishing

Under current conditions, sport fishing is permitted year-round in the Coulee Des Grues along Little California Road. Anglers may harvest any fish species on the refuge that is permitted by state regulations. State fish size and bag limits apply. Creel limits, boating safety, and license requirements are in accordance with state regulations, unless otherwise specified in the fishing brochure. Recreational crawfishing is permitted in designated areas of the refuge from April 1 through May 31. Improving the crawfishery and extending the crawfishing season for the enjoyment of the public were issues identified during the public scoping period and are identified in this plan.

Roads and Trails, Interior and Exterior

In general, lack of access, both interior and exterior, limits all public use on the refuge. No all-weather roads or trails exist.

The refuge has two exterior access routes, Louisiana Highway 1194 and Little California Road. Avoyelles Parish is responsible for maintaining Little California Road, the most direct route from Marksville, Louisiana. Seasonal weather limits access on Little California Road and other interior roads and trails (including that by refuge staff) to 4-wheel-drive and high-clearance vehicles. Access will remain limited until all-weather roads are provided and maintained.

REFUGE ADMINISTRATION

Funding and Staffing

Currently, the refuge is not meeting its waterfowl and shorebird habitat objectives; has few public use facilities; provides few wildlife-dependent environmental education, interpretation, or wildlife viewing opportunities; and has facilities in need of repair (e.g., water control infrastructure, roads, and public access).

IV. Management Direction

INTRODUCTION

The Service manages fish and wildlife habitats considering the needs of all resources in the decision-making process. But first and foremost, fish and wildlife conservation assumes priority in refuge management. A requirement of the National Wildlife Refuge System Improvement Act of 1997 is for the Service to maintain the ecological health, diversity, and integrity of refuges. Public uses are allowed if they are appropriate and compatible with wildlife and habitat conservation. Hunting, fishing, wildlife observation, wildlife photography, and environmental education and interpretation are priority public uses and therefore emphasized in this plan.

Described below is the comprehensive conservation plan for managing the refuge over the next 15 years. This management direction contains the goals, objectives, and strategies that will be used to achieve the refuge vision.

Three alternatives for managing the refuge were considered: Alternative 1, the no-action alternative; Alternative 2 (active management); and Alternative 3 (restoration of endemic ecosystem). Each of these alternatives is described in the Alternatives section of the Environmental Assessment (USFWS 2006). The Service chose Alternative 2 as the management action.

Implementing Alternative 2 will result in refuge lands being protected, maintained, restored, and enhanced for waterfowl, migratory game birds, resident wildlife, shorebirds, wading and marsh birds, and threatened and endangered species. Extensive wildlife and plant census and inventory activities will be initiated to develop the baseline biological information needed to implement active management programs on the refuge.

Refuge management actions will be directed towards achieving the refuge's primary purposes: (1) provide wintering habitat for mallards, pintails, blue-winged teal, and wood ducks; and (2) provide production habitat for wood ducks to meet the goals of the North American Waterfowl Management Plan. In addition, the refuge will be managed to contribute to other national, regional, and state goals for protecting and restoring populations of shorebirds, woodcock, and threatened and endangered species.

Active habitat management will be implemented through water-level manipulations, moist-soil and cropland management, reforestation, and forest management designed to provide a historically diverse complex of habitats that meets the foraging, resting, and breeding requirements of a variety of species. An extensive system of levees, water control structures, and pumps will be updated and used in an effort to provide approximately 2,500 acres of seasonally flooded habitats and 2,700 acres of floodable bottomland hardwood forests for a variety of wetland-dependent species.

Under this alternative, the refuge will continue to seek acquisition of all inholdings from willing sellers within the present refuge boundary. The refuge will seek acquisition of an additional 2,500 to 3,000 acres in the Chatlain Lake Unit within the current acquisition boundary to help meet Louisiana waterfowl step-down objectives. Also, the refuge will use outreach programs and seek partnerships with state, federal, and private landowners. In seeking partnerships with adjacent landowners and hunting clubs, the refuge will use conservation easements and cooperative agreements, and work to promote other federal programs, such as the Wetland Reserve Program, to provide wildlife and soil and water conservation benefits for migratory waterfowl and other wildlife species. Land acquired as part of the refuge will be available for compatible wildlife-dependent recreation.

During the 15-year life of this plan, 125 acres of existing refuge cropland will be reforested to achieve wildlife habitat objectives. A forest management plan, designed to create spatially and specifically diverse bottomland hardwood forests (with little negative effect to waterfowl objectives), will be developed and implemented. The upland forest will be converted and managed in native upland forested species.

Cooperative farming will be used to manage and maintain approximately 2,500 acres of waterfowl habitat, including cropland and moist-soil. As much as 370 acres of unharvested crop and a minimum of 600-800 acres of moist-soil habitat will be provided to meet refuge North American Waterfowl Management Plan wintering waterfowl foraging habitat objectives.

Opportunities for quality wildlife-dependent recreation (e.g., hunting, fishing, wildlife observation, wildlife photography, and environmental education and interpretation) will be provided. Improvements will be made to the refuge's interior and exterior access roads to provide all-weather vehicular access to a broad segment of the public. Opportunities for hiking and all-terrain vehicle use will be provided to support wildlife-dependent recreation to the extent that these activities do not significantly interfere with or detract from the achievement of wildlife conservation. A wildlife observation site and platform, interpretive trails, boardwalk, kiosks, and a demonstration area at the Headquarters' Office area and an exhibit site in the Headquarters' Office will be provided to allow for fully accessible environmental education and interpretation programs. Quality fishing and hunting programs will be provided, consistent with sound biological principles with sufficient focus on waterfowl/waterbird sanctuary, loafing, feeding, and courting requirements. Fishing and crawfishing will be permitted on the refuge. A visitor services plan, incorporating an aggressive and proactive promotion of both on- and off-site programs, will be developed and implemented.

VISION

> *Grand Cote National Wildlife Refuge will provide critical migration habitat in the Mississippi Alluvial Valley for wintering pintail, mallard, blue-winged teal, wood duck, and other waterfowl species through intensive management of agricultural, moist-soil, and forested wetland habitats. Grand Cote Refuge will provide optimal production habitat for wood ducks. Grand Cote Refuge will manage fish and wildlife resources to meet local, state, and national goals while promoting compatible wildlife-dependent recreational opportunities.*

GOALS, OBJECTIVES, AND STRATEGIES

The goals, objectives, and strategies presented are the Service's response to the issues, concerns, and needs expressed by the planning team, the refuge staff and partners, and the public and are presented in hierarchical format. Chapter V, Plan Implementation, identifies the projects associated with the various strategies.

These goals, objectives, and strategies reflect the Service's commitment to achieve the mandates of the National Wildlife Refuge System Improvement Act of 1997, the mission of the National Wildlife Refuge System, and the purposes and vision of Grand Cote National Wildlife Refuge. The Service intends to accomplish these goals, objectives, and strategies within the next 15 years.

Goal A. Wildlife Management. Maintain viable, historically diverse populations of native fish and wildlife species consistent with sound biological principles.

Objective A-1. Migratory Waterfowl. Provide biological framework to meet the population goals of the North American Waterfowl Management Plan as stepped down through the Lower Mississippi Valley Joint Venture, primarily for mallards, pintail, blue-winged teal, and wood ducks.

Discussion: The Mississippi Alluvial Valley is a critical ecoregion for migrating and wintering ducks and geese in North America (Reinecke et al. 1989). The primary purpose of the refuge is to provide important foraging and resting habitats for waterfowl and to serve an integral role in the large, cooperative planning and habitat management effort known as the North American Waterfowl Management Plan.

Concern over waterfowl population declines in the 1980s resulted in establishment of the North American Waterfowl Management Plan, which focused the attention of federal, state, and private conservation groups on critical wintering and breeding areas. The Mississippi Alluvial Valley was selected as one of the wintering habitat focus areas. One of the first tasks faced by the Lower Mississippi Valley Joint Venture was to create a model or decision tool for determining how much habitat was needed and a way to relate this objective to the population goals of the North American Waterfowl Management Plan. The solution was to view wintering areas as responsible for contributing to the spring breeding population goals proportional to the percentage of ducks historically counted in wintering areas (Loesch et al. 1994, Reinecke and Loesch 1996). To contribute ducks to spring populations, wintering areas have to provide sufficient habitat to ensure adequate winter survival. To quantify winter habitat requirements, the Lower Mississippi Valley Joint Venture identified limiting factors and assumed foraging habitat was most likely to limit waterfowl populations in the Mississippi Alluvial Valley (Reinecke et al. 1989).

Guidelines for minimum duck-use-days were developed based on a series of step-down plans starting with population objectives. These foraging requirements were then allocated to each state within the Joint Venture. Within each state, coordination meetings were held to determine who could provide the habitat requirements among management units on public and private lands. Taking into account sanctuary requirements (in addition to foraging requirements), public land managers determined what potential there was to meet state objectives. For Grand Cote National Wildlife Refuge, Joint Venture step-down objectives for the refuge were adjusted based on multi-species, duck life-history requirements (e.g., molting, pairing, courtship, and foraging), other refuge waterfowl (e.g., mallard, pintail, teal, and wood duck) requirements, and a more refined assessment of refuge purposes and capabilities. A current review of North American Waterfowl Management Plan goals and objectives is being undertaken and a revised allocation of duck-use-days will be incorporated as part of this comprehensive conservation plan.

Strategies:

- Continue bi-weekly ground surveys from August through March and mid-winter aerial count. Participate in white goose and Canada goose surveys as appropriate.

- Archive complete digital database of all waterfowl surveys and habitat use. Habitat conditions and waterfowl numbers should be analyzed to determine if preferred habitat conditions throughout the winter period exist. Differences in species habitat preferences, both within and among years, should be recorded, archived, and analyzed over a period of years, and management strategies should be adapted as needed.

- Maintain a core area of at least 2,500 impoundment acres as waterfowl sanctuary. Include units WF001-12, WF19-22, and WF24-27 in the core sanctuary area.

- Review population objectives and compare with actual waterfowl use data at least annually to assure that refuge and landscape-based (e.g., Joint Venture) objectives are being met. Also, complete an assessment on available forage amounts for both grain crop and moist-soil vegetation.

Objective A-2. Nesting/Resident Waterfowl. Provide and expand nesting and brood rearing habitat for wood ducks to support objectives of the North American Waterfowl Management Plan.

Discussion: Wood ducks are year-round residents in the forested wetlands of the United States, including Grand Cote Refuge. Preferred habitats include forested wetlands, wooded and shrub swamps, tree-lined rivers, streams, sloughs, and beaver ponds. Wood ducks seek food in the form of acorns, other soft and hard mast, weed seeds, and invertebrates found in shallow flooded timber, shrub swamps, and along stream banks. They loaf and roost in secluded areas and dense shrub swamps.

Wood ducks are cavity nesters, seeking cavities in trees within a mile of water. Brood survival is higher in situations where nests are close to water. Due to conversion of bottomland hardwood forests to urban sprawl and agriculture, and competition for nest sites from a host of other species, natural cavities are considered to limit reproduction. Nest boxes are commonly used to supplement natural cavities and increase local production of wood ducks. Box programs are not an end to all nesting problems. They require time to clean and repair at least annually. Production can be increased by more frequent checks and cleaning of boxes, but this must be weighed with other time constraints. Currently, over 140 boxes on the refuge are maintained and nest success is monitored. The wood duck nest box program was improved and expanded in 2003 after a biological review of the refuge.

Adequate brood habitat can seriously affect duckling survival and reproductive success. Suitable brood habitat has been improved since 2003 on Grand Cote Refuge. McGilvrey (1968) described preferred brood habitat as 30 to 50 percent shrubs, 40 to 70 percent herbaceous emergents, and 25 percent open water. Due to avian predators, overhead cover within 1 to 2 feet of the water surface is vital for wood duck broods. Optimum habitat should have 75 percent cover and 25 percent open water. Placement of boxes in or adjacent to good brood cover will significantly improve duckling survival to flight stage. This information has been more recently supported by Davis (2001).

One other factor affecting duckling survival is aquatic insect production that is probably poor in highly turbid systems such as Choctaw Bayou and Coulee des Grues. Other than serving as access to good brood habitat (e.g., beaver ponds and oxbow lakes), these waterbodies appear to be relatively poor brood habitat and should not be considered as suitable site for a significant number of nest boxes. However, other portions of the refuge are providing and will provide high-quality brood habitat with proper water management.

The Mississippi Flyway Council has established preseason wood duck banding quotas by state throughout the Mississippi Flyway to estimate survival. Good efforts to meet the refuge complex quota of 150 wood ducks, including age and sex quotas, would significantly contribute to the Council's efforts.

Scrub-shrub and emergent marsh habitat should be developed. Nest boxes should be provided in and adjacent to units as brood rearing habitat develops.

Strategies:

- Expand the nest box program by installing at least 50 new nest boxes with predator guards and consistently maintaining a minimum of 75 nest boxes placed in or adjacent to good brood habitat. Nest boxes should be checked and cleaned at least twice per year, January and August. Add, check, and clean additional boxes as resources allow.

- Maintain and establish suitable brood habitat in Units WF025, WF015, WF017, and WF018, and natural sloughs in the reforested area north of Little California Road.

- Meet or exceed flyway and state banding quotas, including age and sex ratios.

Objective A-3. American Woodcock. Develop and implement forest management plans that include midstory and groundstory vegetation (thickets) in the moist forested lands for daytime cover and foraging habitat in moist agricultural habitats for nighttime foraging by American woodcock. This habitat management will significantly contribute to the American Woodcock Management Plan (U.S. Department of the Interior, Fish and Wildlife Service 1990).

Discussion: American woodcock are migratory game birds that occur throughout the forested portions of the eastern United States. Woodcock populations in this region have declined 19 percent from 1968 to 1990. Population declines are thought to be the result of land-use changes associated with land conversion and the maturing of forested habitats.

In 1990, the American Woodcock Management Plan was completed, setting an objective to protect and enhance winter and migration habitat on public lands to increase woodcock carrying capacity. The plan also set objectives to inventory and monitor woodcock habitat and develop management demonstration areas; however, objectives have not been stepped down to states or individual refuges.

Wintering habitat includes moist bottomland hardwood forests with brush and understory, especially when found in close association with agricultural fields and natural regeneration succession. These sites are typically wet thickets with a high density of plant stems with the ground open and clear. Typical cover includes privet, cane, and briars that results from openings in the canopy. The scrub-shrub and dense habitats found in certain portions of the refuge provide good daytime cover for woodcock. Crepuscular (daytime) cover for woodcock includes thickets and shrub areas with high vertical density in the understory and spongy wet soil. These habitats can be created in existing forest stands through patch group thinning and patch clearcuts that also benefit other high-priority bird species. These habitats result from reforestation, natural regeneration, ice storms, and forest management, all of which are recommended to benefit priority forest interior nesting land birds (e.g., Swainson's warbler and cerulean warbler) and other wildlife.

At dusk, woodcock move to open or brushy fields to forage and conduct courtship activities throughout the night. Preferred nocturnal (nighttime) habitat includes wet agricultural fields (not fall disked) and wet natural regeneration fields or grassland habitats with exposed soil and patchy cover 1 to 3 feet in height created by cool fall burns within 0.5-mile of diurnal habitat. These habitats include agricultural fields that were not fall disked and sparse grasslands that may have received a cool fall burn to create patchy openings of exposed soil interspersed between grass clumps 1 to 3 feet in height. Woodcock are closely tied to earthworms as their major food resource. Mowed or disked strips through reforestation areas will serve as sites for entry into these dense habitats.

Strategies:

- Assess woodcock populations by conducting either evening flight counts, nighttime spotlight counts, or flush counts at least twice monthly from mid-November to mid-March in suitable wintering habitat.

- Develop and implement a forest management plan that includes preferred woodcock habitats.

- Consider conducting cool fall burns in agricultural and fallow fields as a means to create nocturnal habitat.

- Provide open areas or agricultural fields in various stages of plant succession or harvest crop fields for nocturnal habitat.

- Restrict fall plowing by cooperative farming operations to maximize earthworm production in agricultural fields.

- Utilize rights-of-way and other permanent forest openings as a means to provide additional woodcock habitat.

- Develop woodcock habitat demonstration sites to serve as educational opportunities for public and private land managers, realizing that habitat management for woodcock is similar to management for other priority species.

Objective A-4. Marshbirds. Develop and implement habitat management plan that improves freshwater emergent habitat to increase marshbird populations on the refuge.

Discussion: During the last several decades, overall loss of freshwater emergent wetlands has increased from development pressures. This is especially true away from immediate coastlines. King rail, least bittern, pied-billed grebe, American coot, and purple gallinule are species in decline locally and/or regionally due to the loss of freshwater emergent wetlands. All of these species could be present at Grand Cote Refuge. Yellow rail (and possibly black rail) do occur on the refuge and are found in rice fields and early stages of afforestation.

At present, there are no sizeable (>5-acre) patches of tall emergent marsh on the refuge. Most of the potential marshbird habitats do not support tall emergent vegetation. At present, limited resources and the necessary water control and infrastructure does not allow managers to effectively provide this habitat type. It must be recognized that maintenance of tall emergent marsh conditions could be fairly labor intensive due to natural succession of forested habitat.

Grand Cote Refuge would be a good location to support habitat for these and other marshbird species, in conjunction with waterfowl objectives. Studies are needed to determine species composition and abundance on the refuge and if rice fields and other habitats could support breeding marshbird populations.

Strategies:

- Promote tall emergent vegetation to support marshbird breeding populations in Units 15 and 18, along sloughs, and in areas managed to support wood duck brood habitat.

- Initiate basic marshbird surveys to determine use by priority species during the spring and summer. As resources are available, initiate call-back surveys that will contribute to ongoing secretive marshbird surveys consistent with national marshbird protocols.

- Work with U.S. Geological Survey and other partners to initiate research of marshbird use of different habitat types on the refuge.

Objective A-5. Long-legged Wading Birds. Develop and implement a monitoring and habitat management plan that supports nesting and foraging habitat to increase long-legged wading bird populations in conjunction with waterfowl and shorebird habitat management.

Discussion: Generally speaking, nesting long-legged wading birds have plenty of available habitat but the issue of how much disturbance these nesting birds can tolerate is key to protecting the species. At present, no rookeries have been found on the refuge.

Objectives for wood duck brood habitat in flooded willow and buttonbush and promoting early fall shorebird habitat may be sufficient for attracting nesting long-legged wading bird colonies (several colonies presently exist at Lake Ophelia Refuge).

One important aspect of managing for long-legged wading birds, especially wood storks and birds breeding in Mexico, is providing post-breeding foraging habitat in late summer and early fall. Such habitat conditions would involve drawing down water impoundments in late summer, similar to management for shorebirds.

Species of conservation interest in the Mississippi Alluvial Valley include: little blue heron, tricolored heron, yellow-crowned night-heron, wood stork, and white ibis. Daily observations of these species, their numbers, use of impoundments, and the condition and management of the impoundments would provide valuable information for guiding management decisions, in conjunction with use by shorebirds, brooding wood duck, and wintering waterfowl.

Strategies:

- Conduct rookery searches for colonial waterbird species annually and if found, determine species composition, relative abundance, nest status, and if special measures are needed to reduce disturbance.

- Provide late-summer water drawdowns for post-breeding foraging habitat in conjunction with shorebird and moist-soil management activities.

- Determine relative abundance of waders in managed wetlands and flooded agriculture impoundments during post-breeding periods (July -August), concurrently with southbound shorebird surveys.

Objective A-6. Shorebirds. Develop and implement population monitoring and habitat management plans that provide a minimum of 50 acres to support migrating shorebirds as outlined in the Shorebird Conservation Plan.

Discussion: Present Joint Venture step-down objectives for Grand Cote Refuge recommend that 50 acres be provided during southbound migration (July - October). This may actually involve up to 200-300 acres over a season with flood-ups and drawdowns allowing for approximately 50 acres of suitable habitat to be available throughout the migration period.

Opportunities exist for managing shorebirds at Unit 18, in moist-soil units and in fallow crop fields. Providing suitable conditions would include disking dead vegetation and a subsequent schedule of flood-ups and prolonged drawdowns. Alternative management would involve flooding a field from winter through the summer months to provide preferred water depths during the late-July to early-October period. Exposed mudflats grading into 3-4 inches water depth capture the needs of all species. Substantial opportunity exists to work cooperatively with the cannery adjacent to Unit 18 to improve water management capabilities for benefiting all waterbird species.

Strategies:

- Identify potential sites (e.g., impoundments and fallow crop fields) in conjunction with moist-soil management program where newly exposed mudflats can be provided during late-March to late-May and late-July to early-October, rotating among sites as needed to ensure a minimum of 50 acres of available shorebird habitat. Include this information in the habitat management plan.

- Manage Unit 18 for shorebirds and other appropriate species after wood duck brood rearing season and work cooperatively with cannery to improve water management capabilities on the refuge.

- Contribute to International Shorebird Survey by continuing counts in coordination with the South Atlantic Migratory Bird Initiative.

Objective A-7. Species of Special concern. Inventory the distribution and habitat use of all species of special concern, especially the bald eagle, and follow appropriate management/recovery plans to contribute to their recovery.

Discussion: The bald eagle is still listed as a federally threatened species and the southeast regional management guidelines should be followed where nests are established. Currently, bald eagles have not been observed on the refuge.

Strategies:

- Implement Southeast Regional Bald Eagle Management Guidelines, or the most recent update, if any nest sites are found.

- Implement recovery activities as identified in recovery plans or other pertinent documents for listed species that occur on the refuge.

Objective A-8. Neotropical migratory birds. In conjunction with other species management, inventory the distribution and habitat use by neotropical migratory birds, concentrating on early successional bottomland hardwood forest habitat.

Discussion: Many species of songbirds are experiencing long-term declines as a result of widespread habitat loss, particularly bottomland hardwood forests and early successional habitats, such as grasslands and scrub habitats. While the refuge has only 35 acres of mature bottomland hardwood forest, there are 1,186 acres of reforested habitat (currently scrub habitat) and 1,576 acres of natural regeneration that will grow into a mature bottomland hardwood forest. However, this amount of habitat is not large enough to support healthy source populations of certain neotropical migratory bird species and could instead act as a habitat sink.

A large variety of neotropical migratory birds are common in the refuge's different habitats types. Some common year-round residents include the Carolina chickadee, tufted titmouse, northern mocking bird, and red-winged blackbird. Yellow-belled sapsuckers, white-eyed vireo, hermit thrush, yellow-rumped warbler, and white-throated sparrow are some birds common in the winter.

Raptors frequent the fallow fields and reforested areas in search of rodents. Northern harrier, red-shouldered hawk, American kestrel, red-tailed hawk, and Cooper's hawk are some raptors observed on the refuge.

Strategy:

- Conduct Christmas bird counts and winter grassland bird surveys in conjunction with habitat management activities to determine species composition.

Objective A-9. Resident Wildlife (Mammals). Provide quality bottomland hardwood forest, scrub-shrub, and open agricultural areas to sustain healthy and balanced resident wildlife populations.

Discussion: Grand Cote Refuge supports a variety of habitats typical of central Louisiana and, consequently, hosts the full range of wildlife species common to the area. Sound management of the freshwater marshes, agricultural areas, and various other habitats will allow the refuge to maintain current or increase population levels. Population monitoring and a number of control measures can be implemented to provide recreational opportunity and maintain wildlife populations at or slightly below carrying capacity (the population level that can be sustained over the long term by the available habitat).

White-tailed deer are the largest mammals on the refuge and are well adapted to its habitats. Based on general observations, harvest data, and spotlight surveys, deer numbers appear to be low (1 deer to 62 acres). High levels of legal and illegal harvests on private lands may be the causes of low deer numbers. Ordinarily, healthy animals can tolerate the endemic parasites and diseases. With no predators controlling deer population, hunting provides recreational opportunity and is the preferred method to control the deer population. At present, the refuge allows the hunting and harvesting of deer with archery equipment October - January. Deer will continue to be monitored in conjunction with harvests.

Two species of rabbits (e.g., cottontail and swamp) are abundant on the refuge. A recent study showed that both rabbits breed throughout the entire year at this latitude and the number of rabbits produced annually in this type habitat are greater than that of rabbits in more upland habitats. Even though many predators prey on these rabbits, population numbers are thought to be high and at carrying capacity. The annual harvesting of rabbits would have no negative impact on the population and would allow the opportunity for recreational hunting of these under-utilized species.

In Louisiana, animals classified as furbearers include: beaver, bobcat, coyote, gray fox, mink, muskrat, nutria, opossum, river otter, red fox, raccoon, and skunk. Beaver and raccoon populations can reach population levels that may adversely affect ecosystem functions. Beaver have caused deterioration and loss of bottomland hardwoods throughout the refuge.

Excessive numbers of raccoons can cause negative impacts on the reproduction of nongame birds and wild turkeys. Trapping and hunting remain the only viable methods to reduce furbearer population levels. Trapping will be regulated on a permit basis, as needed, to regulate furbearers that are adversely affecting ecosystem functions.

Strategies:

- Integrate key resident species population objectives into habitat management plans.

- Utilize hunting as a tool to manage wildlife populations when it is compatible with other refuge purposes and activities.

- Initiate browse survey working with the Louisiana Department of Wildlife and Fisheries, continue spotlighting surveys, and analyze deer harvest data to monitor the health and density of the deer population. Spotlight surveys estimate deer densities and buck, doe, and fawn ratios.

- Work with adjacent landowners to manage deer populations for the benefit of populations both on and off the refuge.

- Conduct furbearer scent station surveys and general observation surveys to obtain baseline index on predator numbers. Also, monitor and record nuisance wildlife damage and control methods used.

Objective A-10. Nuisance Plant and Animal Control. Control nuisance wildlife and plant populations, especially feral hogs, beaver, nutria, Chinese tallow, Chinese privet, red vine, trumpet creeper, alligator weed, and other exotic and invasive species, as needed, to achieve habitat and population objectives.

Discussion: It is necessary to monitor and, in some situations, control populations of selected wildlife species (e.g., feral pigs and nutria) to protect and benefit native habitats and other wildlife, maintain healthy wildlife populations. Wild pigs are a feral species that cause significant damage to wetlands and habitat. Nutria are an exotic herbivore that can cause significant damage to marsh habitats when populations become elevated, an event referred to as "eat outs." Nutria can be a problem in damaging habitat and levees in some areas. Beavers can plug water control structures making water management for waterfowl impoundments and farming operations difficult.

Some exotic species exist on the refuge and may benefit from current and future management practices. If the uplands are thinned, Chinese tallow and Chinese privet will expand. Inventories are needed to identify non-native plants, their relative abundance, and the most efficient methods of control. The Louisiana State University Cooperative Extension Service can provide useful information on control methods.

Strategies:

- Monitor and document habitat degradation and control beaver and nutria populations as needed to minimize negative habitat impacts.

- Monitor and control feral hog populations to minimize habitat impacts caused by this species. Form a task force to best control feral hog populations.

- Implement an aggressive control program to reduce/eliminate invasive exotic vegetation with an emphasis on control and reduction of Chinese tallow and privet. Integrate this information into a Nuisance Animal and Plant Management Plan.

- Use prescribed burning in conjunction with chemical treatment to control Chinese tallow as needed.

- Seek alternative funding sources and/or mechanisms to address nuisance animal and plant concerns.

- Work with adjacent landowners to encourage participation in control efforts.

- Research/monitor nuisance animal and plant responses to control programs.

Objective A-11. Amphibians and Reptiles. Determine status and habitat associations of reptiles and amphibians at Grand Cote Refuge.

Discussion: Little information exists on amphibians within the Mississippi Alluvial Valley, including the refuge. A recent study was conducted at Lake Ophelia and Tensas River Refuges that provides some potentially useful information, however, a lack of information on species occurrence and habitat use is an issue with these species at Grand Cote Refuge. Thus, there is a need for basic inventory. Some species, such as southern leopard frogs and spring peepers, will potentially benefit from moist-soil management. Other species will require forested wetlands with surrounding forested habitat. In reforestation areas, restoration of sloughs and ephemeral wetlands should be considered. Laser leveling is believed to lead to less suitable anuran breeding habitat in croplands than fields with existing micro-topography, however, as noted above, further study is needed to evaluate the effects of precision leveling on wildlife populations.

Strategies:

- Prepare a Biological Inventory and Monitoring Plan by 2010, which includes inventorying, monitoring, habitat utilization, and standardized data collection procedures for amphibians and reptiles.

- Prepare a Habitat Management Plan by 2009, which identifies and protects essential habitat.

Objective A-12. Fisheries. Manage the crawfish resource to provide a sustainable population for recreational harvest and wildlife.

Discussion: Crawfish are a very important resource to wildlife and the recreational fishing community. The current crawfish season runs through May. Many in the community would like to see an increased season length and production of crawfish on the refuge. By working with specialists in the conservation community, the refuge has the potential to maximize crawfish production.

Strategies:

- Develop a Biological Monitoring and Inventorying Plan by 2010, striving to increase crawfish production in consultation with crawfish specialists; extend season length where appropriate; and monitor crawfish harvest.

- Develop a Water/Habitat Management Plan by 2008, to identify units which will maximize crawfish production for recreational harvest and wildlife.

HABITAT MANAGEMENT

Goal B. Habitat Management. Manage bottomland hardwood and upland forests and moist-soil and cropland habitats to provide a diversity of plant and animal species found in the Mississippi Alluvial Valley.

Objective B-1. Bottomland Hardwood Forests. Protect, restore, and manage 2,797 acres of refuge bottomland hardwood forests, as well as any future acquired forests, to support viable populations of native flora and fauna consistent with sound biological principles and other objectives of this plan.

Discussion: About 80 percent of the original forest lands in the Mississippi Alluvial Valley have been cleared and converted to other land uses, leaving only remnant forested tracts. Fish and wildlife resources have been similarly impacted, leaving remnant populations that must be managed to meet the refuge purpose and to achieve their maximum potential as it relates to landscape-level planning. The refuge may act as a habitat sink for forest interior land birds or the threatened Louisiana black bear due to the small forest patch size and adjacent agricultural and residential lands surrounding the refuge. Therefore, forest resources should be managed primarily to meet the purposes of other refuge resources, particularly wintering waterfowl in the flood-prone areas, woodcock, and resident wildlife.

The refuge currently consists of 1,576 acres of naturally regenerated bottomland hardwoods, 1,186 of reforested bottomland hardwoods, and 35 acres of mature, remnant bottomland hardwood forest. A forest habitat management plan will have to be completed for the refuge before active forest management can begin. Efforts should be focused initially on the existing stands and scrub-shrub areas. Improving and maintaining the red oak component in all stands to 30-50 percent of the stand composition and spot planting specially grown containerized trees (e.g., root pruned or other) to help ensure a hard mast component within a reasonable period of time should be considered and outlined in the management plan.

Greentree reservoirs are impounded bottomland hardwood forests. Placing levees in these bottomlands will often significantly change the natural hydrology and hydroperiod of the impounded lowland forest. Thus, management of greentree reservoirs should attempt to mimic the local, natural, and historical hydrology and hydroperiod under which the forest was established. An ideal scenario might be to match the flooding regime of these reservoirs with the natural and historical frequency, duration, and depth of inundation; however, this approach may not be compatible with waterfowl habitat management objectives and goals of the refuge (i.e., to provide relatively consistent forested wetland habitat for ducks and hunters). Greentree reservoirs in the Mississippi Alluvial Valley are typically managed to be flooded during the waterfowl season from late-November through at least the end of January. The historic hydroperiod probably included annual flooding during a much later period (January through February) on an annual basis, with flooding beginning as early as mid-November and extending into May or June in some years. This variable flood period maintained a healthy, diverse forest structure and should be mimicked to the degree possible. A constant hydroperiod that follows the waterfowl hunting season results in a less healthy forest that favors only the few species benefited by the static hydrologic regime.

Strategies:

- Complete a basic forest inventory, including species composition, survival, growth, and density of all forested and greentree reservoir sites on the refuge.

- Develop a forest/habitat management plan that promotes at least a 30 percent red oak component by 2008.

- Establish GIS database/habitat types of the refuge forests, including mitigation sites to be used in future habitat management activities.

- Reforest an additional 125 acres of open areas into appropriate bottomland hardwood tree species.

- Develop a water/habitat management plan that establishes and monitors water regimes to mimic natural flooding conditions of forests or greentree reservoirs by 2008.

- Develop a water control infrastructure to manage greentree reservoir areas using the best management practices developed.

- Manage habitats to support woodcock populations.

Objective B-2. Upland Forest Management. Convert 273 acres of upland forested area to native upland hardwoods.

Discussion: Currently, 273 acres of upland forest consists primarily of offsite and nonnative species. During the 2003 Biological Review, the team identified native upland species appropriate for this area. The principal native upland hardwood trees for the loess soils should be cherrybark oak, water oak, and sweetgum. The upland prairie terrace soils should be mixed hardwood and pine forest. The Biological Review recommended a thorough inventory of the area, soil survey, and management to control and eliminate nonnative species.

Strategies:

- Complete a basic forest inventory of all upland areas, including species composition, survival, growth, density, and volume.

- Utilizing forest inventory, develop a forest/habitat management plan by 2008, using best management options; convert existing 273-acre pine upland forest to a native upland hardwood forest.

- Control Chinese tallow and Chinese privet as needed by mechanical, burning, or chemical control methods.

Objective B-3. Waterfowl Impoundment Management/Moist-soil. Manage 600-800 acres of moist-soil habitat for wintering waterfowl to meet North American Waterfowl Management Plan step-down objectives for Louisiana.

Discussion: Moist-soil management propagates natural, wetland plants that produce seeds or tubers high in protein and other nutrients that are a seasonally important component of the diets of migrating waterfowl. Cover created in most moist-soil units is also a crucial habitat component for ducks, particularly during the pair-bonding period. Invertebrates found in these sites, which are high in protein, are also utilized by migratory waterfowl.

The timing of drawdowns in waterfowl impoundments on the refuge to propagate moist-soil plants has ranged from mid-March, for annual smartweed production, to late-June to maximize sprangletop and barnyard grass production. Water depth in the surrounding bayou/coulee is another factor that determines the drawdown schedules. Most drawdowns conducted are considered slow at approximately 3" per week.

Some common desirable moist-soil plants found in impoundments are annual smartweed, sprangletop, red rooted sedge, and wild millets (e.g., barnyard grass and jungle rice). Estimated pounds/acre of seeds for these moist-soil plants (Laubhan 1992) have ranged from 252 to 588 pounds per acre (minus red rooted sedge; with red rooted sedge = 403 - 19,297 pounds/acre) in moist-soil sites on the refuge during 2002 and 2003 growing seasons. Red vine, alligator weed, coffeeweed, cocklebur, button bush, and willow trees are some common nuisance plants found in moist-soil units on the refuge. Disking, flooding, herbiciding, and rotating moist-soil plants with Japanese millet are common practices used when nuisance plants become a problem. Generally, units are disked and planted to millet at least every 3 years for nuisance plant control.

Fall flooding for wintering waterfowl, in a typical year, begins around late-November or early-December and is usually rain-dependent. Impoundments are generally flooded at half capacity during this time and gradually the water is raised until full capacity around late-January, making food available to waterfowl as the water rises. The water is generally dropped gradually after this time period to concentrate invertebrates for waterfowl. Pumping early water (September) in impoundments is generally conducted in a few areas each year for shorebirds and teal, but is not common due to expense.

Strategies:

- Provide a minimum of 600 to 800 acres of moist-soil habitat. In order to maximize moist-soil production, 25 percent of the acreage may be alternated annually between cropland, moist-soil, and shorebird habitat.

- Develop a water/habitat management plan by 2008, with specific management strategies and target species outlined to maximize moist-soil production. The goal should be to produce a minimum of 400 pounds per acre of preferred waterfowl food or at least 50 percent coverage of good to preferred waterfowl plants in all moist-soil areas annually.

- Monitor moist-soil units periodically throughout the growing season, keeping records of all management actions, water levels, etc., by management unit. Develop GIS database for all moist-soil impoundments that quantifies seed production, water regimes, and vegetation response to management actions (e.g., burning, mowing, and disking) to maximize food production.

- Adapt management strategies to improve food production and waterfowl usage of the food resources produced on the refuge.

- Develop and promote a partnership with the research community to evaluate the most effective waterfowl habitat management strategies.

- Develop better water-control infrastructure to manage moist-soil impoundments.

Objective B-4. Waterfowl Impoundment Management/Cropland. Manage 1,850 acres of cropland habitat for wintering waterfowl using cooperative farming to help meet North American Waterfowl Management Plan step-down objectives for Louisiana.

Discussion: Grain production is an important component of the refuge meeting its waterfowl foraging habitat objective. At this time, cooperative farming is the only option available to producing crops. Rice, milo, and corn are the top choices as grain crops for ducks in the Mississippi Alluvial Valley. Rice is particularly resistant to decomposition even under flooded conditions. Milo and corn also provide high-energy resources for waterfowl and can generally be kept above the water surface, but problems arise from depredation prior to flooding, as well as seed degradation after flooding. Soybeans can also be grown, although not the preferred crop by managers because of the rapid decomposition after flooding and low protein absorption by waterfowl.

Cooperative farming has been and will continue to be a cost-effective mechanism to provide the high-quality "hot foods" required by wintering waterfowl. Management of a cooperative farming program not only reduces dependence on refuge staff and equipment, it also creates jobs and infuses money into the local economy.

Strategies:

- Maintain current level of crop production to provide a diversity of high-carbohydrate (hot) foods as flooded habitat required by migrating and wintering waterfowl. Provide as much as 370 acres of unharvested rice and milo to meet foraging habitat objectives.

- Grain crops, such as rice, milo, or corn, should be provided as the preferred waterfowl foods; however, due to economic or environmental circumstances, soybeans may be grown as an alternative crop/food source.

RESOURCE PROTECTION

Goal C. Resource Protection. Conserve natural and cultural resources through partnerships, protection, and land acquisition from willing sellers.

Objective C-1. Land Protection Needs. Focus acquisitions on inholdings within the current refuge boundary and wetland/agricultural lands within the Chatlain Lake Unit of Grand Cote Refuge acquisition boundary to meet overall management objectives and improve access.

Discussion: In 1989, the Grand Cote Refuge boundary was established and consisted of 13,000 acres divided equally among the Choctaw Bayou and Chatlain Lake units. The first fee title acquisition occurred in 1993, when approximately 6,000 acres were purchased from The Nature Conservancy. Little emphasis has been placed on the remaining lands within the Chatlain Lake unit largely due to limited resources.

There are several parcels of land that lie within the existing refuge boundary that are not owned by the Service. Several of these parcels compromise management due to conflicting management purposes and disturbance to wildlife. Acquisition/exchange of these parcels would eliminate access issues, improve management options, and tighten some unclear and confusing boundary issues.

As a result of the Biological Review, it was determined that Grand Cote Refuge is not meeting its waterfowl objectives. A renewed emphasis should be placed on the Chatlain Lake acquisition area, with land purchases in large enough blocks to realistically and practically make management of this area possible.

Strategies:

- Assess inholdings, consult private landowners within current refuge boundary, and acquire land from willing sellers.

- Develop inventory of current land ownership within the Chatlain Lake unit and contact landowners to discuss Service land acquisition programs.

- Purchase between 2,500 and 3,000 acres of agricultural/wetland habitats to meet waterfowl habitat objectives.

Objective C-2. Private Land Conservation. Restore and maintain native biodiversity, improve water quality, and enhance migratory waterfowl habitat on private lands surrounding the refuge in the Mississippi Alluvial Valley through use of land incentive programs.

Discussion: Most of the land in the Mississippi Alluvial Valley is privately owned and must play an important role in the restoration and maintenance of native biodiversity achieving the goals and objectives of national wildlife refuges and national and regional plans, such as the North American Waterfowl Management Plan, Partners in Flight, Mississippi River Alluvial Valley Bird Conservation Plan, etc. In an effort to address those objectives, the Service established a private lands program known as Partners for Fish and Wildlife. Through this program, the Service provides technical assistance and delivers financial assistance programs to private landowners. Support to Grand Cote Refuge is provided by private lands biologists stationed at Bayou Cocodrie National Wildlife Refuge and the Service's Lafayette, Louisiana, Ecological Services Field Office.

The regional Partners for Fish and Wildlife Program also provides financial assistance to landowners wishing to restore wetlands. Landowners are limited to $25,000 of financial assistance per year. In the Mississippi Alluvial Valley, most projects involve the restoration of hydrology and hardwood reforestation. Vegetation, up to 30 percent of the area, can be manipulated to maintain successional stages other than what would be expected to occur naturally. For example, up to 30 percent of the area could be managed as moist soil.

A concerted effort to pull together a partnership, including local communities and agencies, such as the USDA's Natural Resources Conservation Service and Farm Service Agency, and the Department of Environmental Quality, will be required to affect land use practices throughout the watershed to have a significant impact on aquatic resources downstream of the refuge.

Strategy:

- Work with private lands biologists to deliver a variety of programs that provide technical and financial assistance necessary to help achieve migratory bird goals and objectives on private lands.

Objective C-3. Watershed Management. Complete a hydrological assessment and water quality baseline to maximize benefits to waterfowl, shorebirds, and other native flora and fauna. Work with local, state, and federal partners to aid the restoration of hydrology on the refuge and surrounding lands where applicable.

Discussion: Prior to its establishment, the area encompassing the refuge was intensively farmed and a series of man-made levees, irrigation ditches, pumps, and water control structures were constructed to facilitate farming in flood prone areas. Most of those structures are still present on the refuge today, and are used to manage water for waterfowl and shorebirds. The natural hydrology of the area, however, has been altered by those structures. In addition to the structures, the refuge uses a limited amount of laser land leveling on some cooperatively farmed fields, which produces uniform topography and influences hydrology. Removal of, or modifications to, some of those structures may reestablish more natural hydrologic regimes onto portions of the area; however, those modifications could impact other refuge management currently in place, such as cooperative farming and waterfowl management.

In addition to onsite structures, flood control measures off-refuge, including the Chatlain Lake Canal, Spring Bayou dam, channalization of Coulee des Grues, and the Red River levee system, have also impacted historic hydrologic regimes. Extensive land clearing for agriculture off-refuge has also increased sediment, nutrient, and contaminant inputs into Choctaw Bayou and Coulee des Grues, and into other water bodies located outside of the refuge. Additionally, effluent from a cannery located on the refuge boundary may periodically degrade refuge water quality.

The Army Corps of Engineers, Avoyelles Wildlife Federation, and Avoyelles Parish Police Jury are currently investigating potential solutions to water quality and sediment deposition problems experienced in the Spring Bayou area of the parish. The Avoyelles Parish Flood Hazard Mitigation Plan addresses these issues specifically *(Kisatchie-Delta Regional Planning and Development District, Inc., 2003)*. This area lies east of the refuge and receives input from Coulee des Grues. The Corps has developed several alternatives to address Spring Bayou's water quality problems. The preferred alternative includes: installation of an inlet structure through the Red River levee at Choctaw Bayou along with a 200-cubic-foot-per-second pump to reestablish flows from the Red River into the bayou; control structures on Bayou du Lac and Coulee des Grues to reduce sediment inputs into the Spring Bayou area; clearing and snagging the channels in Choctaw Bayou and Coulee des Grues; dredging portions of several water bodies located outside the refuge for flow conveyance; and modification of an existing weir. Those actions listed above have the potential for direct and indirect impacts to the refuge's hydrology and water quality. Water quality would be expected to improve with reintroduction of Red River inputs. Amount and frequency of backwater flooding on the refuge could be altered by the proposed control structure on Coulee des Grues and by downstream dredging.

A thorough analysis of existing hydrology on the refuge is necessary in aiding water management decisions and in predicting the impacts of off-refuge aquatic restoration or flood-control actions.

Strategies:

- Work with the Natural Resources Conservation Service, Army Corps of Engineers, and Ducks Unlimited to complete a hydrological evaluation of existing refuge conditions, and to examine the potential beneficial and negative impacts from any proposed land grading, irrigation system modification or installation, wetland construction, levee breaching, etc., on the refuge.

- Investigate/establish water quality baseline for the refuge. Coordinate with Louisiana Department of Environmental Quality to determine if sampling sites on the refuge are needed.

- Work with partners to restore the hydrology of the refuge where applicable and in the best interest of the Service, and contribute to the health of the entire watershed, utilizing the refuge hydrological assessment, refuge water quality baseline survey, and plans such as the Avoyelles Parish Flood Hazard Mitigation Plan, the Spring Bayou Restoration Plan, and other resulting studies. Ensure that opportunities for fish and wildlife habitat are enhanced and do not materially detract from the purposes of the refuge.

- Work with the Allen Canning Company and Louisiana Department of Environmental Quality to improve water quality in its oxidation ponds. Investigate strategies for enhanced shorebird, waterfowl, and marsh bird management on the ponds.

- Integrate water quality and watershed protection into water management plan.

Objective C- 4. Cultural Resources. Identify and protect cultural and historic resources and minimize disturbance or inadvertent damage that could occur as a result of management activities.

Discussion: The Tunica-Biloxi Indian Tribe, located in Avoyelles Parish, has an association with the area and can be a valuable partner in any efforts to protect, study, and interpret these sites.

Strategies:

- Develop a comprehensive archaeological survey of all refuge lands that includes a digital GIS layer.

- Develop a partnership with the Tunica-Biloxi Indian Tribe to interpret the significance of the refuge's archaeological sites to Native Americans and the general public if applicable.

- Comply with all regulations and policy set forth in the National Historic Preservation Act, Archaeological Resources Protection Act, and Native American Grave Protection and Repatriation Act.

VISITOR SERVICES

Goal D. Visitor Services. Develop and implement a quality wildlife-dependent recreation program that leads to a greater understanding and appreciation of fish and wildlife resources and enjoyable recreational experiences.

Objective D-1. Visitor Services Program. Develop and improve visitor access, facilities, and program support to promote priority wildlife-dependent recreational uses.

Discussion: The National Wildlife Refuge System Improvement Act of 1997 identifies six priority wildlife-dependent public use activities: hunting, fishing, wildlife observation, wildlife photography, and environmental education and interpretation. Fundamental to the provision of these uses are viable and diverse fish and wildlife populations and the habitats upon which they depend. These priority uses, along with all other proposed uses, must be compatible with the refuge purpose and the mission of the National Wildlife Refuge System. The proposed visitor facilities are illustrated in Figures 9 and 10.

Strategies:

- Develop and implement a visitor services plan by 2008.

- Utilize the recreational fee program to maintain and enhance visitor facilities, (i.e., interpretive information, waterfowl hunting blinds, fishing pier, bank fishing areas, and trail access).

- Promote youth education through participation in the Youth Conservation Corp Program.

- Use consistent signage at all visitor service areas (e.g., parking, hiking, hunting, fishing, and all-terrain vehicles).

- Place standardized refuge information in parking areas.

- Develop small exhibit area in the current Headquarters' reception area.

- Seek refuge road funding in partnership with Avoyelles Parish to improve Little California Road and provide signage and informational kiosks where needed.

- Develop outdoor interpretive area outside Headquarters' Office and host a kids fishing day in new pond.

- As use increases, improve parking areas (e.g., gravel and add bumpers).

- Expand the volunteer program to help implement the Visitor Services Program.

- Work with interested community members/volunteers to create a Friends Group for the refuge complex.

Objective D-2. Hunting. Provide safe, quality hunting opportunities in appropriate areas consistent with the refuge's established purposes and wildlife and habitat objectives for 1,000 visitors.

Discussion: Hunting, when conducted under carefully controlled conditions, is not detrimental to most wildlife populations. In addition, hunting is an opportunity to participate in one of the identified priority wildlife-dependent recreational uses. Development of a hunt plan, based on sound biological information, is a vital component for assuring quality hunting experiences and viable wildlife populations.

Hunting on newly acquired lands will be conducted in accordance with refuge purposes reflected in the authorizing legislation and Refuge System policy. If lands within the current refuge acquisition boundary are acquired, the number of hunting opportunities and hunting visits could be increased.

Figure 10. Current and planned hunting and fishing visitor facilities on Grand Cote National Wildlife Refuge

Hunting seasons will be scheduled and managed to ensure that negative effects to non-game wildlife and migratory birds are minimized during critical periods. Hunting seasons will be set in close coordination with the Louisiana Department of Wildlife and Fisheries.

Strategies:

- Increase youth hunt opportunity and participation (e.g., Green-wing Program) with partners such as Ducks Unlimited and others.

- Open new space blind waterfowl hunting areas in Units 13, 14, and 23.

- Evaluate hunting schedule and consider increasing waterfowl hunting opportunities.

- Open more areas to deer hunting as additional lands are acquired.

- Evaluate and consider offering special dove hunting opportunities for youth, women, and disabled hunters.

Objective D-3. Fishing. Provide quality crawfishing opportunities in Units 13, 14, 17, 19, and 20, and bank fishing along the Coulee Des Grues for 2,500 visitors.

Discussion: Sport fishing is permitted year-round in the Coulee Des Grues along Little California Road. Anglers may harvest any fish species on the refuge that is permitted by state regulations. State fish size and bag limits apply. Creel limits, boating safety, and license requirements are in accordance with state regulations unless otherwise specified in the fishing brochure. Recreational crawfishing is permitted in designated areas of the refuge with pyramid nets from April 1 through May 31. The harvest is limited to 100 pounds per permit holder per day. No commercial crawfishing is permitted. All crawfishing gear, including nets, boats, bait, and trash, must be removed from refuge property after each visit.

Strategies:

- Expand crawfish season duration in areas not affected by waterfowl management and open new areas as opportunities allow.

- Provide all-weather vehicle and universally accessible facilities (e.g., gravel roads, piers, and bank fishing areas).

Objective D-4. Wildlife Observation and Photography. Develop and provide opportunities and facilities for wildlife observation and photography with emphasis on areas near the Headquarters' Office.

Discussion: On the north and south sides of Little California Road there are more than 10 miles of trails along the levees that could be opened to hiking and wildlife observation. There is a short trail at the headquarters area with a new boardwalk and observation tower, which was constructed in 2006.

Waterfowl can be seen during the winter months and migratory songbirds, shorebirds, and wading birds can be seen during the spring and summer.

Strategies:

- After the duck hunting season, permit the use of blinds for photography and wildlife observation on a reservation basis.

- Coordinate with area schools and other organizations to utilize boardwalk and observation tower off Headquarters' trail loop using interpretive panels and spotting scope to view wildlife.

Objective D-5. Environmental Education. Develop a community-based environmental education program in coordination with area schools and other area educational organizations.

Discussion: There is no environmental education occurring at the refuge and none of the current staff have any background or training in environmental education. There are three high schools, two middle schools, and two elementary schools in Avoyelles Parish. There is also one charter school and several parochial schools in the parish. There is a very large school system in the city of Alexandria, which is less than an hour's drive from the refuge. There is also a zoo and a Children's Tree House Museum in the Alexandria area. There are some information panels at the zoo, which describe the Service's mission.

Strategies:

- Look for existing educational programs, such as the Alexandria Zoo and Tree House Children's Museum, and provide information and opportunities that exist on the refuge to contribute to these programs.

- Hire an intern to create self-guided "kits" for teachers to use on Headquarters' trail and/or field area.

- Work with teachers in the community to help develop programs for the refuge (e.g., junior duck stamp, science, wood duck box program, and junior refuge manager).

- Establish relationship with parish school system (and adjacent parishes – Alexandria/Pineville area), familiarize staff with state education standards, and incorporate into refuge programs. Develop and implement an environmental education plan, which includes on- and off-site educational opportunities, curriculum and support materials, and support facilities.

Objective D-6. Environmental Interpretation. Develop an interpretive program that will increase awareness of the habitat features, wildlife values, and management programs on the refuge.

Discussion: There are no interpretive panels anywhere on the refuge. There is a need for a trained interpretive specialist. There are some taxidermy mounts in the Headquarters' reception area.

Strategies:

- Create a demonstration area at the Headquarters' Office (e.g., gardening for wildlife or backyard habitat or native plant landscape) and create a new pond in the field area.

- Provide appropriate interpretation panels at all observation sites, including the boardwalk and observation tower. Include panels depicting cultural history of the area in partnership with local tribe.

- Develop exhibit site at Headquarters' Office.

- Develop interpretive trail guide for Headquarters trail emphasizing bird identification and refuge purposes and management activities (e.g., crop lands, water management, and reforestation).

Objective D-7. Law Enforcement. Maintain highly trained and effective law enforcement personnel to ensure trust resource protection, visitor safety, and enforcement of all refuge-related acts and regulations.

Discussion: Protecting the natural resources of the refuge and ensuring the safety of refuge visitors are fundamental responsibilities of the Refuge System. This refuge is accomplishing this responsibility with one full-time officer. As crime continues to increase in rural America, refuges face a larger and more complicated enforcement problem. In addition to natural resource violations, serious felonies, including homicides, rapes, assaults, and acts of arson, are occurring on refuges every year.

Strategies:

- Provide up-to-date training and equipment to all full-time and dual function officers.

- Develop Memorandums of Understanding with state and parish law enforcement agencies to facilitate cooperation and assistance in law enforcement activities. Update current law enforcement plan.

- Provide education and outreach programs in the local community as part of a preventive law enforcement effort.

- Provide assistance to the Service's special agents and state conservation officers for off-refuge activities as requested.

REFUGE ADMINISTRATION

Goal E. Refuge Administration. Develop short- and long-term staffing needs for Grand Cote Refuge that are necessary to meeting objectives set forth in establishing legislation, step-down plans, mission, etc.

Objective E-1. Staffing and Budget Needs. Work with the Regional Office to identify critical staffing and budget needs that are realistically possible within the next 10 to 15 years.

Discussion: Currently, there is only one temporary employee dedicated to the management of Grand Cote Refuge. Other complex staff members, as assigned, contribute to the management of the refuge; however, maintenance personnel do not routinely report to Grand Cote Refuge and there is only excess and reassigned equipment available for use unless a timely transfer of equipment from Lake Ophelia Refuge occurs. Funding of two positions in the short term, sharing of three additional positions in the long term, and acquisition of a large tractor and disk will substantially increase the refuge's ability to meet its management obligations.

The managers at the Central Louisiana National Wildlife Refuge Complex face a series of challenges in managing a cooperative farming program and enhancing and maintaining productivity of moist-soil impoundments at Grand Cote Refuge. An overarching issue is the need for additional biological staff to plan and supervise management activities and adequate technical staff to implement field operations. The refuge currently has a biologist and manager that are shared with the other refuges in the complex. One temporary maintenance worker is assigned to Grand Cote Refuge. One tractor is assigned specifically to this refuge. As a minimum, there is a need for a manager/biologist, maintenance worker/equipment operator, and biotech, all of whom would be working with the cooperative farmers and other refuge personnel when available. The refuge needs a large tractor and farm equipment (e.g., heavy plow, spray rig, seed drill, and mower, as a minimum) to facilitate habitat management at the level recommended in this plan. It is recommended that the refuge have one employee for every 300-400 acres of moist-soil habitat, at least on a seasonal basis.

Strategies:

- Develop a short- and long-term staffing plan.

- Seek resources to purchase fundamental equipment necessary to perform wetland and waterfowl management objectives.

- Utilize the Student Temporary Experience Program to support refuge programs.

- Convert the temporary maintenance position to a permanent maintenance position with at least 50 percent of duties to support public use.

- Establish assistant refuge manager position.

- Support additional new shared positions identified in the Comprehensive Conservation Plan for Lake Ophelia National Wildlife Refuge, such as wildlife biologist, forester, outdoor recreation planner, park ranger, and maintenance worker.

V. Plan Implementation

INTRODUCTION

Congress has distinguished a clear legislative mission of wildlife conservation for all national wildlife refuges. National wildlife refuges, unlike other public lands, are dedicated to the conservation of the nation's fish and wildlife resources and not wholly dedicated to recreational uses. Priority projects emphasize the protection and enhancement of fish and wildlife species first and foremost, but considerable emphasis is placed on balancing the needs and demands for recreation and environmental education.

To accomplish the purpose, vision, goals, and objectives contained in this plan for Grand Cote National Wildlife Refuge, this section identifies projects and a cost summary, funding and personnel needs, volunteers, partnerships opportunities, step-down management plans, and a monitoring and adaptive management plan, and plan review and revision.

PROJECTS

Listed below are the project summaries and their associated costs for baseline data collection and interpretation, exotic species control, habitat restoration and management, land protection, facility development and maintenance, and staffing over the next 15 years. This project list reflects the priority needs identified by the public, planning team, and refuge staff based upon available information. These projects were generated for the purpose of achieving the refuge's objectives and strategies (Table 3). The primary linkages of these projects to those planning elements are identified in each summary.

Table 3. Summary of Grand Cote National Wildlife Refuge Comprehensive Conservation Plan projects.

Project #	Description	First Year Cost	Recurring Annual Cost	Staff FTE's
Existing Budget Base				10 FTE
1	Science-based Monitoring and Inventory	See Lake Ophelia NWR CCP	See Lake Ophelia NWR CCP	
2	Control Invasive Feral Swine	$30,000	$15,000	
3	Water Management System Operation	$420,000	$95,000	1
4	Water Management System Maintenance	$60,000	$55,000	1
5	Waterfowl Impoundment/Moist-soil Habitat Inventory and Management	$158,000	$20,000	
6	Forest Inventory, Reforestation, and Habitat Management	$85,000	$15,800	
7	Heavy Equipment Package	$340,000	$20,000	

Project #	Description	First Year Cost	Recurring Annual Cost	Staff FTE's
8	Control Invasive Plants	$15,000	$15,000	
9	Land Protection	$5-15 million*	*	
10	Boundary Line Surveys and Posting	$200,000	$3,000	
11	Archaeological Surveys	$123,000	$3,000	
12	Visitor Services Program	$100,000	$5,000	
13	Visitor Contact Areas	$350,000	$20,000	
14	Upgrade Administrative Roads	$2.8 million***	$6,000	
15	Little California Road Partnership	$2.05 million	$7,000	
16	Gates and Refuge Entry	$24,500	$500	
17	Maintenance Facilities	$49,500	$5,000	
18	Vehicle Replacement	$75,000	$75,000	
19	Staff Housing	$250,000	$25,000	
Grand Total		$7,130,000	$385,300	2**

* Cost not included in grand total and recurring costs unknown at this time.
** Two additional positions are needed in addition to the 5 new positions identified in the Lake Ophelia National Wildlife Refuge Comprehensive Conservation Plan that would also support Grand Cote National Wildlife Refuge.
*** Cost projection for Project 14 will take place over the 15-year life of this final plan.

FISH AND WILDLIFE POPULATION MANAGEMENT

Project 1: Science-based Inventory and Monitoring of Plant and Animal Populations

Science-based inventories and monitoring of plant and animal populations are critical to ensuring the biological integrity of the refuge. Information collected will serve as the basis for developing habitat management plans and will influence all management activities. A systematic inventory and monitoring program will enable the refuge to make informed management decisions and valuable long-term contributions to national and regional objectives for waterfowl, shorebirds, wading birds, wintering forest and scrub-shrub birds, and resident wildlife. Standardized census and survey techniques will be employed and all data compiled into databases, including GIS for spatial analysis. This information is critical to formulating management actions and evaluating wetland restoration, habitat utilization, trends analysis for migratory and resident wildlife, and other programs. All data will be shared with appropriate state and federal partners in an effort to further ecosystem management. This project supports the wildlife biologist position identified in the Comprehensive Conservation Plan for Lake Ophelia National Wildlife Refuge. The estimated first year cost for this project is encapsulated within the Lake Ophelia Refuge CCP. *(Linkages: Lake Ophelia Refuge CCP, Goal 1, Objectives 1-9; Goal 4, Objectives 1, 2, and 5, and Grand Cote Refuge CCP Goal A, Objectives A-1-A-12.)*

Project 2: Control Invasive Feral Swine

Grand Cote Refuge has an established population of feral swine. The scientific literature has documented many adverse effects caused by feral swine on the habitat productivity and reproduction of native wildlife. Being omnivores, feral swine utilize virtually every component of the habitat and directly compete with native wildlife, reducing their carrying capacity and adversely affecting their reproduction and recruitment. Feral swine are compromising the refuge's efforts in wetland restoration, reforestation, and habitat management. Currently, the refuge is using a multi-faceted control program, including public hunting, staff control, trapping, and various other techniques described in the Reducing Wildlife-Caused Damage Plan. This project will provide professional animal damage control personnel to supplement the refuge staff's feral swine control efforts. Control work will be contracted with USDA Wildlife Services and/or other professional nuisance animal control personnel. The estimated first-year cost of this project is $30,000, with a recurring cost of $15,000. *(Linkages: Goal A, Objectives A-1-A-12; Goal B, Objectives B-1-B-4.)*

HABITAT MANAGEMENT

Project 3: Water Management System Operation

Man-made hydrological alterations have all but eliminated the natural flooding regimes that once supported historical numbers of waterfowl and shorebirds. In this altered floodplain, a system of levees, water control structures, and wells are necessary to provide dependable flooded habitats that correspond with the migration chronologies of migratory birds. The timing of water management is critical to meet the needs of migratory birds, the primary purpose of the refuge, to stimulate the production of desirable moist-soil plants and to control undesirable plants. Water management includes monitoring water flow, water levels, and pumping via a GIS database to more efficiently manage resources. This project will increase water management capabilities by 1,500 acres. To efficiently improve, manage, and maintain the water management system, this project includes the installation or replacement of additional water control structures ($50,000), two irrigation wells and power units ($150,000), one low lift pump ($40,000), and an underground irrigation pipe system ($50,000). This project will add one permanent assistant manager position and vehicle to support position ($130,000 first-year cost, $75,000 recurring). The estimated first-year total cost of this project is $420,000, with a recurring cost of $95,000. *(Linkages: Goal A, Objectives A-1 and A-2; Goal B, Objectives B-3 and B-4).*

Project 4: Water Management System Maintenance

The refuge uses a system of levees, water control structures, and wells in an effort to mimic historic flooding regimes and provide dependable flooded habitat for migratory birds. This system consists of approximately 27 waterfowl impoundments, 20 miles of levees, 36 water control structures, 7 wells, and 3 lift pumps. The refuge can provide over 2,500 acres of managed seasonal flooding with this water management system. For the functional operations of the entire water management system to work reliably, annual maintenance must be performed on the levees, water control structures, wells, and power units. This project includes monitoring equipment maintenance, water flow, water levels, pumping, etc., via GIS and other databases to more efficiently manage resources. This project will provide a permanent maintenance worker to perform annual maintenance ($52,269). The total estimated first-year cost of this project is $60,000, with a recurring cost of $53,000. *(Linkages: Goal A, Objectives A-1 and A-2; Goal B, Objectives B-3 and B-4.)*

Project 5: Waterfowl Impoundment - Moist-soil Habitat Inventory and Management

A habitat management program will become increasingly important if the refuge is to contribute to regional and national goals for migratory birds. An all-inclusive habitat inventory will be developed and implemented to create a digital habitat map. A habitat management plan will be developed. Waterfowl management activities will include management of moist-soil habitat, which requires disking every 2 to 3 years and/or rotation to Japanese millet to maintain desirable plant composition. This project supports 2 positions in the Lake Ophelia Refuge CCP, the refuge operations specialist and the wildlife biologist. This project will supply the necessary equipment (180-hp tractor and disc, $100,000; six-row planter, $10,000; row conditioner, $12,000; seed drill, $15,000; spray boom, $6,000; and 15-foot flex-wing bush hog, $15,000) to manage habitats on the refuge. The estimated first-year cost of this project is $163,000, with a recurring cost of $20,000, and the remaining costs are included within Projects 1, 6, and 7 of the Lake Ophelia Refuge CCP. (*Linkages: Lake Ophelia Refuge CCP Goal 2, Objectives 1 and 2; Grand Cote Refuge CCP Goal B, Objectives B-1-B- 4.*)

Project 6: Forest Habitat Inventory, Reforestation, and Management

This project will allow an extensive inventorying and monitoring of current bottomland hardwood and upland forest habitat. This project will ensure that existing reforestation and natural regeneration areas will be evaluated and replanted as appropriate, approximately 125 acres of surplus cropland will be reforested, and 273 acres of upland forest will be replanted to native species. An active forest management program will become increasingly important if the refuge is to contribute to regional and national goals for migratory birds, woodcock, and resident wildlife. The development and implementation of a forest management plan is critical to the health and maintenance of the forested habitat. This project supports 2 positions identified in the Lake Ophelia Refuge CCP. Project estimates include funding for evaluation, monitoring, equipment, planting materials, and contracted tree planting. The estimated cost of evaluation and reforestation is $85,000 over the next 15 years ($14,000 for current reforestation and natural regeneration (2,762 acres) evaluation and replanting, $25,000 to reforest 125 acres, and $54,000 to reforest 273 acres of upland forest). Recurring costs associated with fire suppression, monitoring, and management will average $5 per acre per year or $15,800 and the remaining costs are included within Projects 6 and 7 of the Lake Ophelia Refuge CCP. (*Linkages: Lake Ophelia Refuge CCP Goal 2, Objectives 1 and 2; Grand Cote Refuge CCP Goal B, Objectives B-1 and B-2.*)

Project 7: Heavy Equipment Package

This project will complete essential rehabilitation work on over 28 miles of roads and trails, 20 miles of levees, and annual habitat management in moist-soil waterfowl impoundments. It will include installation or replacement of water control structures; building or repairing levees; purchases of essential heavy equipment to complete rehabilitation and development projects; the removal of woody vegetation from roads, ditches, and levee shoulders; and biannual disking and rehabilitation of moist-soil impoundments. This work, along with the needed heavy equipment, is critical for restoring the refuge's hydrology, meeting waterfowl objectives, and enhancing its accessibility to the public. Necessary equipment includes a heavy crosscutting disk ($20,000); 175 hp tractor ($80,000); a Gorilla tree cutter ($15,000); backhoe ($75,000); a bulldozer ($150,000); and use of heavy equipment identified in the Lake Ophelia Refuge CCP. The estimated first-year cost of this project is $340,000, with an annual recurring cost of $20,000. (*Linkage: Goals A-E.*)

Project 8: Control Undesirable Vegetation

The refuge's biological integrity is threatened by a variety of invasive plant species. This project will develop and implement an integrated pest management program to control invasive and undesirable plants. Invasive and undesirable plant occurrence will be mapped and quantified. Appropriate strategies will be used to control alligator weed, coffeeweed, cocklebur, Johnsongrass, water primrose, redvine, and trumpet creeper in moist-soil and cropland impoundments; and Chinese tallow trees in reforestation and upland forest areas. Strategies will include chemical, mechanical, and biological control techniques ($15,000). This project will support the resource specialist position identified in the Lake Ophelia Refuge CCP. The estimated cost is $15,000, with a recurring cost of $15,000 per year, and the remaining costs identified in the Lake Ophelia Refuge CCP. *(Linkages: Lake Ophelia Refuge CCP Goal 1, Objective 1, Goal 2, Objectives 3-5, and Goal 4, Objectives 1 and 2; and Grand Cote Refuge CCP Goal A-B.)*

RESOURCE PROTECTION

Project 9: Land Protection

Through a combination of fee title purchases from willing sellers and leases, and cooperative agreements and conservation easements with willing landowners, the Service will continue to purchase inholdings within the existing Choctaw Bayou Unit and 2,500-3,000 acres in the Chatlain Lake approved acquisition boundary to meet Louisiana step-down waterfowl habitat objectives. The Service will acquire sufficient interest in the identified lands to prevent conflicting land uses and to provide the management flexibility required to protect and manage the habitat as a national wildlife refuge. Additionally, this project will eliminate numerous small inholdings and consolidate refuge boundaries, eliminating many administrative and public access issues. The acquired lands will be made available to the public for additional wildlife-dependent recreation. All acquisitions will be made from willing sellers. Potential funding sources for this project include the Migratory Bird Conservation Fund, Land and Water Conservation Fund, carbon sequestration and cooperative efforts with various Service partners. The estimated cost of this project is $5-15 million. *(Linkage: Goal C, Objective C-1.)*

Project 10: Boundary Line Surveys and Posting

Several portions of the current refuge boundary have not been surveyed and other portions have inadequate field points that preclude accurate boundary delineation. Registered surveys provide a legally defensible boundary line that is critical to resource protection and public relations, especially with regard to adjacent landowners. This project will fund surveys for approximately 40 miles of boundary line at an estimated cost of $5,000 per mile. The total cost of this project is $200,000, with a recurring cost of $3,000. *(Linkages: Goal C, Objectives C-1 and C-3; Goal D, Objective D- 1.)*

Project 11: Archaeological Survey

A comprehensive archaeological survey of Grand Cote Refuge will be conducted in coordination with the local Native American tribe. This project is essential to meet federal cultural resource mandates and will provide the baseline information needed for protection of existing archaeological and cultural resources and resource/public use development activities. The estimated first-year cost of this project is $123,000, with a recurring cost of $3,000. *(Linkage: Goal C, Objective C-3.)*

Project 12: Visitor Services Program

Currently, Grand Cote Refuge offers limited opportunities for wildlife-dependent recreation due primarily to a lack of facilities and availability of staff to plan and implement a visitor services program. This project will support an outdoor recreation planner identified in the Lake Ophelia Refuge CCP to develop, organize, and implement an overall visitor services program that will include hunting, fishing, wildlife observation, wildlife photography, and environmental education and interpretation. It will also support an office clerk position identified in the Lake Ophelia Refuge CCP to handle public use related phone calls, process hunt applications, sell permits, and distribute brochures. Directional and interpretive signs will be developed and placed throughout the refuge to accommodate all types of wildlife-dependent visitation. Programs and tours will be developed and provided to schools and other interested groups. Facilities will be developed for persons with disabilities. Some of the first-year costs are included in the Lake Ophelia Refuge CCP. In addition, the estimated first-year cost of this project is $100,000, with a recurring cost of $5,000. *(Linkage: Goal D, Objectives D-1-D-6.)*

Project 13: Visitor Contact Areas

A wildlife interpretation/demonstration area will be developed surrounding the Headquarters Office. An exhibit area, including refuge orientation, will be developed at the Headquarters Office. Site-specific areas will also be developed for public information throughout the refuge. Each site will include maintained trails with boardwalks, foot bridges (when necessary), interpretive panels, and observation blinds or platforms. Informational brochures and interpretive panels will describe the area's natural and cultural resources, management programs, and the Refuge System. The estimated cost of this project is $350,000, with a recurring cost of $20,000. *(Linkage: Goal D, Objectives D-3-D-7.)*

Project 14: Upgrade Administrative Roads

The primary access roads throughout the refuge waterfowl management area are constructed of dirt. These roads are used on a daily basis to transport equipment, monitor the water management system, and perform associated maintenance activities. The roads become impassable during wet weather and hinder refuge management. Upgrading them will consist of shaping the road beds, adding culverts, and applying 6 inches of gravel. This project will ensure dependable all-weather access to perform critical refuge operations and allow the development of compatible wildlife-dependent recreation in other areas of the refuge. The estimated cost of this project is $2.8 million, with a recurring cost of $6,000. *(Linkages: Goal D, Objectives D-3-D-7; Goal E, Objective E-1.)*

Project 15: Little California Road Partnership

Poor access on Little California Road severely hampers public opportunities to visit and enjoy Grand Cote Refuge. Currently, Little California Road is one of the primary means of access to most wildlife-dependent recreational uses on the refuge. This road has very little gravel, floods during heavy rain events, and has poor drainage making it impassable during wet weather. This project will partner with the Avoyelles Parish Police Jury, who owns the surface right-of-way of the road, to reconstruct the road to minimum public use standards by raising the road beds, adding drainage culverts, and resurfacing with gravel. Funding for road construction will be requested from the TEA-21 Refuge Roads fund and partnering with the Avoyelles Parish Police Jury ($50,000). The total estimated cost of this project is $2.05 million, with an annual recurring cost of $7,000. *(Linkage: Goal D, Objectives D-1-D-7.)*

Project 16: Refuge Entry and Gates

Currently, the refuge has little ability to restrict access to areas not open to the public in order to protect resources. Poaching and trespassing into these areas where the refuge would like to minimize disturbance to wildlife resources has often been a problem. Installing seven entry gates in certain closed areas would help protect resources and reduce poaching and disturbance. The total estimated cost to purchase and install seven gates is $24,500, with an annual recurring cost of $500. *(Linkage: Goal D, Objectives D-1-D-7.)*

REFUGE ADMINISTRATION

Project 17: Maintenance Facilities

Currently, refuge maintenance fleet and Service vehicles are unprotected outside of the Headquarters Office. Equipment, boats, and other important materials are stored in areas accessible to the public. The refuge is in urgent need to construct a pole barn ($30,000) and security fence ($19,500) to maintain and protect equipment. The estimated cost of this project is $49,500, with a recurring cost of $5,000. *(Linkage: Goal E, Objectives E-1)*

Project 18: Vehicle Replacement

Refuge operations, maintenance, and law enforcement depend on reliable vehicles capable of travel both on- and off-road. The refuge uses a combination of trucks, vans, ATVs, and boats for access. These vehicles are subjected to rough terrain and severe duty that effectively shorten their serviceable condition to less than 5 years. The refuge needs to replace, on average, at least two vehicles every 5 years and one ATV every third year to maintain a safe and dependable vehicle fleet. The estimated cost of this project is $75,000, with a recurring cost of $75,000 every two or three years. *(Linkage: Goal E, Objectives E-1.)*

Project 19: Staff Housing

Effective refuge management is contingent on science-based planning and monitoring. The refuge relies and works closely with universities, U.S. Geological Survey, and others to continually improve management based on science. Many of the refuge wildlife surveys and monitoring programs are conducted by interns who are paid $30/day. The need to provide a bunkhouse to shelter interns and students conducting research is paramount to making critical management decisions. The estimated cost of this project is $250,000, with a recurring cost of $25,000. *(Linkage: Goal A, Objectives A-1-A-12; Goal E, Objective E-1)*

FUNDING AND PERSONNEL

Currently, a staff of ten permanent positions has been approved for the refuge complex and must share duties and responsibilities between the Lake Ophelia, Grand Cote, and Cat Island National Wildlife Refuges.

To complete the extensive wildlife habitat management and restoration projects and conduct the necessary inventorying, monitoring, analysis, and mapping activities, more staff is required. The addition of two new positions will enable the refuge to achieve its plan objectives and strategies within a reasonable time. The annual cost of operating the entire Refuge Complex in addition to two new positions (including salaries and benefits) will be $1.31 million.

VOLUNTEERS/PARTNERSHIP OPPORTUNITIES

A major objective of this comprehensive conservation plan is to establish partnerships with local volunteers, landowners, private organizations, and state and federal natural resource agencies. In the immediate vicinity of the refuge, opportunities exist to establish partnerships with sporting clubs, elementary and secondary schools, and community organizations. At regional and state levels, partnerships might be established or enhanced with organizations such as the Louisiana Department of Wildlife and Fisheries, Roy Martin Lumber Company, Bayou State Bowhunters, The Nature Conservancy, Ducks Unlimited, National Audubon Society, Ruffed Grouse Society, Avoyelles Wildlife Federation, Avoyelles Parish Planning Commission, Quality Deer Management Association, and National Wild Turkey Federation.

The volunteer program and other partnerships that could be generated will depend upon the number of staff positions the Service provides the refuge. As staff and resources are committed to the refuge, opportunities to expand the volunteer program and develop partnerships will be enhanced.

STEP-DOWN MANAGEMENT PLANS

A comprehensive conservation plan is a strategic plan that guides the direction of the refuge. Before some of the strategies and projects can be implemented, detailed step-down management plans will need to be prepared or updated and implemented. To assist in preparing and implementing the step-down plans, the staff will develop partnerships with local agencies and organizations. These plans (Table 4) will be developed in accordance with the National Environmental Policy Act, which requires the identification and evaluation of alternatives and public review and involvement prior to their implementation.

Table 4. Grand Cote National Wildlife Refuge step-down management plans related to the goals and objectives portion of the Comprehensive Conservation Plan

Plan	Completion Date
Habitat Management	2009
Moist-soil/Water Management	2008
Forest Management	2008
Cropland Management	2008
Integrated Pest Management	2009
Nuisance Animal Control	2008
Exotic Plant Control	2008
Fire Management	2011
Visitor Services	2010
Environmental Education	2010
Fishing	2009

Plan	Completion Date
Hunting and Trapping	2008
Wildlife Observation and Photography	2009
Law Enforcement	2010
Biological Inventory/Monitoring Plan	2010

Note: Plans are shown in sequence according to goals and objectives listed in Chapter IV of this plan.

Habitat Management Plan (Develop), Draft Completion 2009: This plan will describe the overall desired habitat conditions needed to fulfill refuge purpose and objectives. The plan will include three sections dealing with moist-soil/water-management units, forests, and croplands. Procedures, techniques, and time tables for achieving desired conditions will be developed into an overall plan.

- **Moist-soil/Water-Management Plan** (Update), Draft Completion 2008: This plan will describe the strategies and procedures (timing and duration of flooding and disturbance) for manipulating the refuge's water management units to meet habitat management objectives.

- **Forest Management Plan** (Develop), Draft Completion 2008: This plan will describe strategies for meeting refuge forest management objectives. It will include direction on reforestation, stand improvement, and harvest. Also, scrub-shrub habitat management will be addressed.

- **Cropland Management Plan** (Update), Draft Completion 2008: This plan will describe management of refuge agricultural lands. It will identify what crops will be grown, rotations, mechanical methods, chemical use, rent agreements, and how the program will meet wildlife management objectives.

Integrated Pest Management Plan (Develop and Update), Draft Completion 2009: This plan will address the complex issue of bringing exotic and nuisance plants and animals to a maintenance control level on the refuge. It will cover chemical pesticide use (aerial and ground application), mechanical eradication, and biological controls. The Nuisance/Exotic Animal and Plant control plans will be sections of this plan.

- **Nuisance Animal Control Plan** (Update), Draft Completion 2008: This plan (as part of the Integrated Pest Management Plan) will describe survey, removal or control, and monitoring techniques for both terrestrial and aquatic nuisance and exotic animals (vertebrate and invertebrate). Feral swine and beaver control will be included in this plan.

- **Exotic Plant Control Plan** (Develop), Draft Completion 2008: This plan (as part of the Integrated Pest Management Plan) will describe survey, removal or control, and monitoring techniques for both terrestrial and aquatic nuisance and exotic plants.

Fire Management Plan (Update), Draft Completion 2011: This plan will describe wild and prescribed fire management techniques that will be employed on the refuge. Wildfire control descriptions will include initial attack strategies and cooperative agreements with other agencies. Little reliance on prescribed fire is expected and its use will consist of burning brush piles, irrigation ditches, agricultural stubble, etc.

Visitor Services Plan (Develop), Draft Completion 2010: This plan will describe the refuge's wildlife-dependent recreation, and environmental education and interpretation. Specific issues or items that will be addressed include facility requirements, site plans, and handicapped accessibility. The environmental education, fishing, hunting, and sign plans will be sections of this plan.

- **Environmental Education Plan** (Develop), Draft Completion 2010: This plan (as part of the Visitor Services Plan) will reflect the objectives and strategies of the comprehensive conservation plan and address environmental education guidelines following Service standards.

- **Fishing Plan** (Update), Draft Completion 2009: This plan (as part of the Visitor Services Plan) will address specific aspects of the refuge's fishing program. It will define season structures, fish areas, methods, handicapped accessibility, facilities needed, and refuge-specific regulations.

- **Hunting and Trapping Plan** (Update), Draft Completion 2008: This plan (as part of the Visitor Services Plan) will address specific aspects of the refuge's hunting program. It will define species to be hunted/trapped, season structures, hunt areas, methods, all-terrain vehicle use, handicapped accessibility, facilities needed, and refuge-specific hunting regulations.

- **Wildlife Observation and Photography Plan** (Update), Draft Completion 2009: This plan (as part of the Visitor Services Plan) will describe the refuge's strategy for informing visitors via signage. It will incorporate Service guidelines.

Law Enforcement Plan (Update), Draft Completion 2010: This plan will provide a reference to station policies, procedures, priorities, and programs concerning law enforcement.

Biological Inventory/Monitoring Plan (Develop), Draft Completion 2010: This plan will describe inventory and monitoring techniques and time frames. All plant communities and associations in the refuge, as well as all trust species (migratory birds, including songbirds, neotropical migratory birds, and waterfowl), listed species (federal and state threatened, endangered, and species of concern), and key resident species shall be inventoried, and population trends will be monitored. These data are essential to guide the management of wildlife populations, habitat, and wildlife-dependent public use on the refuge.

MONITORING AND ADAPTIVE MANAGEMENT

Adaptive management is a flexible approach to long-term management of biotic resources that is directed over time by the results of ongoing monitoring activities and other information. More specifically, adaptive management is a process by which projects are implemented within a framework of scientifically driven experiments to test the predictions and assumptions outlined within a plan.

To apply adaptive management, specific surveying, inventorying, and monitoring protocols will be adopted for the refuge. The habitat management strategies will be systematically evaluated to determine management effects on wildlife populations. This information will be used to refine approaches and determine how effectively the objectives are being accomplished. Evaluations will include ecosystem team and other appropriate partner participation. If monitoring and evaluation indicate undesirable effects for target and non-target species and/or communities, then alterations to the management projects will be made. Subsequently, the comprehensive conservation plan will be revised. Specific monitoring and evaluation activities will be described in the step-down management plans.

PLAN REVIEW AND REVISION

This comprehensive conservation plan will be reviewed annually to determine the need for revision. A revision will occur if and when conditions change or significant information becomes available, such as a change in ecological conditions or a major refuge expansion. The plan will be augmented by detailed step-down management plans to address the completion of specific strategies in support of the refuge's goals and objectives. Revisions to the comprehensive conservation plan and the step-down management plans will be subject to public review and NEPA compliance.

Appendix I. Glossary

Adaptive Management

A process in which projects are implemented within a framework of scientifically driven experiments to test predictions and assumptions outlined within the comprehensive conservation plan. The analysis of the outcome of project implementation helps managers determine whether current management should continue as is or whether it should be modified to achieve desired conditions.

Alternative

Alternatives are different means of accomplishing refuge purposes, goals, and objectives and contributing to the National Wildlife Refuge System. An alternative is a reasonable way to fix the identified problem or satisfy the stated need.

Approved Acquisition Boundary

A project boundary which the Director of the Fish and Wildlife Service approves upon completion of the detailed planning and environmental compliance process.

Biological Diversity

The variety of life and its processes, including the variety of living organisms, the genetic differences among them, and the communities and ecosystems in which they occur. The National Wildlife Refuge System focus is on indigenous species, biotic communities, and ecological processes.

Biological Integrity

The biotic composition, structure, and functioning at genetic, organism, and community levels comparable with historic conditions including the natural biological processes that shape genomes, organisms, and communities.

Canopy

A layer of foliage, generally the upper-most layer, in a forest stand. The term can be used to refer to mid- or under-story vegetation in multi-layered stands. Canopy closure is an estimate of the amount of overhead tree cover (also referred to as canopy cover).

Categorical Exclusion

A category of actions that does not individually or cumulatively have a significant effect on the human environment and has been found to have no such effect in procedures adopted by a federal agency pursuant to the National Environmental Policy Act of 1969.

CFR

Code of Federal Regulations.

Compatible Use	A wildlife-dependent recreational use or any other use of a refuge that, in the sound professional judgment of the refuge manager, will not materially interfere with, or detract from, the fulfillment of the mission or the purposes of the refuge. A compatibility determination supports the selection of compatible uses and identifies stipulations or limits necessary to ensure compatibility.
Comprehensive Conservation Plan	A document that describes the desired conditions of the refuge; provides long-range guidance and management direction for the refuge manager to accomplish the purposes, goals, and objectives of the refuge; and contributes to the mission of the National Wildlife Refuge System and meet relevant mandates.
Conservation Easement	A legal document that provides specific land-use rights to a secondary party. A perpetual conservation easement usually grants conservation and management rights to a party in perpetuity.
Cooperative Agreement	A simple habitat protection action in which no property rights are acquired. An agreement is usually long-term and can be modified by either party. Lands under a cooperative agreement do not necessarily become part of the National Wildlife Refuge System.
Corridor	A route that allows movement of individuals from one region or place to another.
Cover Type	The present vegetation of an area.
Cultural Resources	The remains of sites, structures, or objects used by people of the past.
Cypress and Tupelo Swamp	Found in low-lying areas–swales and open ponds–that hold water several months, if not all of the year. Large hollow trees are used as bear den sites.
Deciduous	Pertaining to perennial plants that are leafless for some time during the year.
Dominant Tree	Tree whose canopy is above height of main forest canopy. Crown receives full sunlight on at least three sides.
Ecological Succession	The orderly progression of an area through time in the absence of disturbance from one vegetative community to another.
Ecosystem	A dynamic and interrelating complex of plant and animal communities and their associated non-living environment.

Ecosystem Management	Management of natural resources using system-wide concepts to ensure that all plants and animals in ecosystems are maintained at viable levels in native habitats and that basic ecosystem processes are perpetuated indefinitely.
Emergent Tree	Tree whose height is well above main forest canopy height. It may be a relic from previous forest stand or a faster growing species of same age class.
Endangered Species	A plant or animal species listed under the Endangered Species Act that is in danger of extinction throughout all or a significant portion of its range.
Endemic Species	Plants or animals that occur naturally in a certain region and whose distribution is relatively limited to a particular locality.
Even-Aged Forests	Forests that have two or fewer age classes of trees.
Environmental Health	The composition, structure, and functioning of soil, water, air, and other abiotic features comparable with historic conditions, including the natural abiotic processes that shape the environment.
Environmental Assessment	A concise document, prepared in compliance with the National Environmental Policy Act, which briefly discusses the purpose and need for an action, as well as alternatives to such action, and provides sufficient evidence and analysis of impacts to determine whether to prepare an environmental impact statement or finding of no significant impact.
Fauna	All the vertebrate and invertebrate animals of an area.
Federal Trust Species	All species for which the federal government has primary jurisdiction, including federally threatened or endangered species, migratory birds, anadromous fish, and certain marine mammals.
Fee-title	The acquisition of most or all of the rights to a tract of land. There is a total transfer of property rights with the formal conveyance of a title. While a fee title acquisition involves most rights to a property, certain rights may be reserved or not purchased, including water rights, mineral rights, or use reservation (the ability to continue using the land for a specified time period, or the reminder of the owner's life).

Finding of No Significant Impact	A document prepared in compliance with the National Environmental Policy Act, supported by an environmental assessment that briefly presents why a federal action will have no significant effect on the human environment and states that an environmental impact statement, therefore, will not be prepared.
Floodplain Woods	Bottomland hardwood forests. Consists of hardwoods (old growth and mid-succession-age timber) and cypress tupelo stands found on low ridges that drain slowly and are subject to flooding. Group includes overcup, willow, water oaks, sweetgum, and green ash. Old growth trees typically exceeding 120 years of age. Red oaks were removed in the 1940s. Mid-succession trees are logged timber that may need restoration to improve wildlife habitat.
Fragmentation	The process of reducing the size and connectivity of habitat patches. The disruption of extensive habitats into isolated and small patches.
Goal	Descriptive, open-ended, and often broad statement of desired future conditions that conveys a purpose but does not define measurable units.
Geographic Information System	A computer system capable of storing and manipulating spatial data.
Ground Story (flora)	Vascular plants less than one meter in height, excluding tree seedlings.
Habitat	The place where an organism lives. The existing environmental conditions required by an organism for survival and reproduction.
Herbaceous Wetland	Land annually or seasonally inundated with vegetation consisting primarily of grasses, sedges, rushes, and cattail.
Historic Conditions	The composition, structure, and functioning of ecosystems resulting from natural processes that we believe, based on sound professional judgment, were present prior to substantial human-related changes to the landscape.
Indicator Species	A species of plant or animals that is assumed to be sensitive to habitat changes and represents the needs of a larger group of species.
Inholding	Privately owned land inside the boundary of a national wildlife refuge.

Issue	Any unsettled matter that requires a management decision.
Migratory	The seasonal movement from one area to another and back.
Moist-soil Management	The technique of using water management structures in seasonally flooded impoundments to stimulate the production of natural plant species on exposed mudflats by regulating the timing of water removal in the spring.
Monitoring	The process of collecting information to track changes of selected parameters over time.
National Environmental Policy Act of 1969	A federal law that requires all agencies, including the Service, to examine the environmental impacts of their actions, incorporate environmental information, and use public participation in the planning and implementation of all actions. Federal agencies must integrate this Act with other planning requirements, and prepare appropriate policy documents to facilitate better environmental decision-making.
National Wildlife Refuge	A designated area of land, water, or an interest in land or water within the National Wildlife Refuge System.
National Wildlife Refuge System	Various categories of areas administered by the Secretary of the Interior for the conservation of fish and wildlife, including species threatened with extinction. The Refuge System includes all lands, waters, and interests therein administered by the Secretary as wildlife refuges, wildlife ranges, game ranges, wildlife management areas, or waterfowl production areas.
Native Species	Species that normally live and thrive in a particular ecosystem.
Neotropical Migratory Bird	A bird species that breeds north of the United States/Mexican border and winters primarily south of that border.
Objective	An objective is a concise quantitative (where possible) target statement of what will be achieved. Objectives are derived from goals and provide the basis for determining management strategies. Objectives should be attainable and time-specific.
Planning Area	A planning area may include lands outside existing planning unit boundaries that are being studied for inclusion in the unit and/or partnership planning efforts. It may also include watersheds or ecosystems that affect the planning area.

Planning Team	A planning team prepares the comprehensive conservation plan. Planning teams are interdisciplinary in membership and function. A team generally consists of the a planning team leader; refuge manager and staff biologists; staff specialists or other representatives of Service programs, ecosystems or regional offices; and state partnering wildlife agencies as appropriate.
Preferred Alternative	This is the alternative determined by the decision maker to best achieve the refuge purpose, vision, and goals; it contributes to the Refuge System mission, addresses the significant issues, and is consistent with principles of sound fish and wildlife management.
Purpose of the Refuge	The purpose of the refuge is specified in or derived from the law, proclamation, executive order, agreement, public land order, donation document, or administrative memorandum establishing, authorizing, or expanding a refuge and refuge unit.
Refuge Operating Needs System	This is a national database which contains the unfunded operational needs of each refuge. Projects included are those required to implement approved plans and meet goals, objectives, and legal mandates.
Refuge Purposes	The purposes specified in or derived from the law, proclamation, executive order, agreement, public land order, donation document, or administrative memorandum establishing, authorizing, or expanding a refuge, refuge unit, or refuge subunit.
Selection Harvesting	Form of uneven-age management where individual trees or groups of trees are removed during a harvesting operation.
Seral Forest	A forest in the mature stage of development, usually dominated by large, old trees.
Sink	A habitat in which local mortality exceeds local reproductive success for a given species.
Sink Population	A population in a low-quality habitat in which the birth rate is generally less than the death rate and population density is maintained by immigrants from source populations.
Source	A habitat in which local reproductive success exceeds local mortality for a given species.
Source Population	A population in a high-quality habitat in which birth rate greatly exceeds death rate and the excess individuals leave as migrants.

SPOA	Source Population Objective Area.
Step-Down Management Plans	Step-down management plans provide the details necessary to implement management strategies and projects identified in the comprehensive conservation plan.
Strategy	A specific action, tool, or technique or combination of actions, tools, and techniques used to meet unit objectives.
Threatened Species	Species listed under the Endangered Species Act that are likely to become endangered within the foreseeable future throughout all or a significant portion of their range.
Timber Stand Improvement	Refers to intermediate stand treatment in even-age stands to improve stand characteristics.
Trust Species	Species for which the Fish and Wildlife Service has primary responsibility, including most federally listed threatened and endangered species, anadromous fish once they enter the inland coastal waterways, and migratory birds.
Understory	Any vegetation with canopy below or closer to the ground than canopies of other plants.
Uneven-Aged Forest	Forests that has three or more age classes of trees.
Wildlife Corridor	A landscape feature that facilitates the biologically effective transport of animals between larger patches of habitat dedicated to conservation functions. Such corridors may facilitate several kinds of traffic, including frequent foraging movement, seasonal migration, and the once-in-a-lifetime dispersal of juvenile animals. These are transition habitats and need not contain all the habitat elements required by migrants for long-term survival or reproduction.
Wildlife-Dependent Recreation	A use of a refuge involving hunting, fishing, wildlife observation, wildlife photography, and environmental education or interpretation. The National Wildlife Refuge System Improvement Act of 1997 specifies that these are the six priority general public uses of the Refuge System.

Appendix II. References and Literature Cited

Avoyelles Parish Planning Board. 1947. Avoyelles Parish Resources and Facilities. Louisiana: Department of Public Works Planning Division.

Baron, Jill. 1980. Vegetation impact by feral hogs: Gulf Islands National Seashore, Mississippi. Proc. Second Conf. Sci. Res. Natl. Parks, 8:309-318.

Beccasio, A.D., A.E. Redfield, R.L. Frew, W.M. Levitan, and J.E.Smith. 1983. Lower Mississippi Valley ecological inventory user's guide and information base. USFWS, Division of Biological Services. FWS/OBS-83-19. 84 pp.

Belden, R.C., 1972. Roosting and wallowing activities of the European wild hog (Sus scrofa) in the mountains of East Tennessee. M.S. Thesis, Univ. Tenn.,68 pp.

Belden, R.C. and M.R. Pelton. 1976. European wild hog rooting in the Mountains of East Tennessee. Proc. Annu. Conf. Southeast Assoc. Game & Fish Comm., 29:665-671.

Combs, K.C. 1982. United States Army Corps of Engineers, Briefing: Environmental Defense Fund vs Prevost, US Court of Appeals, Western District of Louisiana.

Cooper, R.J. and R.P. Ford. 1993. Productivity and abundance of Neotropical migratory birds in bottomland hardwood forests of the Mississippi alluvial valley. Annual Progress Report, Memphis State University, Memphis, Tennessee. 11pp.

Cox, R.R., Jr., and A.D. Afton. 1996. Use of habitats by female northern pintails wintering in southwestern Louisiana. J. Wildl. Manage. 61(2):435-443.

Cox, R.R., Jr., and A.D. Afton. 1998[a]. Evening flights of female northern pintails from a major roost site. Condor 98:810-819.

Cox, R.R., Jr., A D. Afton, and R.M. Pace. 1998b. Survival of female northern pintails wintering in southwestern Louisiana. J. Wildl. Manage. 62(4):1512-1521.

Cronk, J.K., and M.S. Fennessy. 2001. Wetland plants: biology and ecology. Lewis Publishers, Boca Baton, Florida, USA.

Davis, J.B. 2001. Survival, recruitment, and management of box-nesting wood ducks in Mississippi and Alabama. PhD Dissertation. MS State Univ. 185 pp.

Davis, J.B., S.E. Stevens, B.D. Leopold, R.M. Kaminski, and P.D. Gerard. 1999. Wood duck reproduction in small and large nest boxes in Mississippi: a continued experiment. Proc. of the annual conference of the Southeastern Fish and Wildlife Agencies 53:257-269.

Fisk, H.N. 1940. Geology of Avoyelles and Rapides Parishes. Geological Bulletin No. 18. Department of Conservation, Louisiana Geological Survey. New Orleans, LA. 239 pp.

Fredrickson, L.H. and M.E. Heitmeyer. 1988. Waterfowl Use of Forested Wetlands of the Southern United States: An Overview. Pages 307-323 in M.W. Weller, editor. Waterfowl in Winter. University of Minnesota Press, Minneapolis, Minnesota.

Fredrickson, L.H., and D.L. Batema. n.d. Greentree Reservoir Management Handbook. Gaylord Memorial Laboratory Wildlife Management Series, Number 1. Gaylord Memorial Laboratory, The School of Natural Resources, Univ of Missouri-Columbia, Puxico, MO. 85pp.

Fredrickson, L.H., and T.S. Taylor. 1982. Management of seasonally flooded impoundments for wildlife. U.S. Fish and Wildlife Service Resource Publication 148, Washington, DC, USA.

Fredrickson, L.H. 1996. Moist-soil management, 30 years of field experimentation. International Waterfowl Symposium 7:168-177.

Gibson, J.L. 1989. Cultural Resources Survey of Seven Proposed Plug Levee Construction Areas, Lake Ophelia National Wildlife Refuge and Voinche/Brouillette Farmers' Home Administration Tract, Avoyelles Parish, Louisiana. Submitted to U.S. Fish and Wildlife Service, Southeast Region, Atlanta.

Hamel, P.B. 1992. The Land Manager's Guide to the Birds of the South. The Nature Conservancy and the United States Department of Agriculture Forest Service. Atlanta, Georgia.

Helmers, D.L. 1992. Shorebird management manual. Western Hemisphere Shorebird Reserve Network. Manomet, MA 58 pp.

Hunter, B.E. 2000. Wood duck use rates of small versus large nest boxes. MS Thesis. Louisiana State University.

Hunter, C. B., and Golder. In prep. Draft of the Southeast U.S. Waterbird Conservation Plan. USFWS, Atlanta, GA.

Hunter, W.C., D.N. Pashley and R.E.F. Escano.1992. Neotropical migratory landbirds species and their habitats of special concern within the Southeast region. Pages 159-169 in D.M.

Jacobi, J.D. 1980. Changes in a native grassland in Haleakala National Park following disturbance by feral pigs. Proc. Second Conf. Sci. Res. Natl. Parks, 8:294-308.

Jones, Dennis, and Malcolm Shuman. 1989 *Archaeological Atlas and Report of Prehistoric Indian Mounds in Louisiana*. Vol. IV Avoyelles Parish, Part 1. Museum of Geoscience, Louisiana State University, Baton Rouge.

Jones, Dennis, and Malcolm Shuman. 1990 *Archaeological Atlas and Report of Prehistoric Indian Mounds in Louisiana*. Vol. V Avoyelles Parish, Part 2. Museum of Geoscience, Louisiana State University, Baton Rouge.

King, S. 2000. Personal Communication, May, 2000. U.S. Geological Survey, Biological Resources Division, Lafayette, LA.

Lacki, M.J. and R.A. Lanica. 1986. Effects of wild pigs on beech growth in Great Smokey Mountains National Park. J. Wildl. Manage. 50(4):655-659.

Laubhan, M. 1992. A technique for estimating seed production of common moist-soil plants. Waterfowl Management Handbook, Fish and Wildlife Leaflet 13.4.5, Washington, D.C.

Lipscomb, D.J. 1989. Impacts of feral hogs on longleaf pine regeneration. South. J. Appl. For. 13(4):177-181.

Lichtenberg, J.S. 2000. Personal communication. May 1, 2000. U.S. Geological Survey, Biological Resources Division. Lafayette, LA.

Loesch, C. R., D. J. Twedt, K. Tripp, W. C. Hunter, and M. S. Woodrey. Development of Management Objectives for Waterfowl and Shorebirds in the Mississippi Alluvial Valley in R. Bonney, D. N. Pashley, R. J. Cooper, and L. Niles, eds. 1999. Strategies for Bird Conservation: The Partners in Flight Planning Process. Cornell Lab of Ornithology.

Loesch, C.R., K.J. Reinecke, and C.K. Baxter. 1994. Lower Mississippi Valley Joint Venture Evaluation Plan. U.S. Fish and Wildlife Service, Lower Mississippi Valley Joint Venture, Vicksburg, Mississippi, USA.

Louisiana Cooperative Extension Service. 1999. Louisiana Summary of Agriculture and Natural Resources. Baton Rouge, LA: Louisiana State University.

Louisiana Department of Agriculture and Forestry, Office of Forestry. 1999. Landowner Income From Sale of Timber, Louisiana and Parishes. Baton Rouge, LA.

Louisiana Department of Economic Development. 1998. "Avoyelles Parish Profile." Louisiana Electronic Assistance Program.

Louisiana Department of Economic Development, Bureau of the Census. 2000. "Avoyelles Parish Profile." Louisiana Electronic Assistance Program.

Louisiana Department of Economic Development. 2004. "Avoyelles Parish Profile." Louisiana Electronic Assistance Program.

Louisiana Department of Environmental Quality. 1998. Water Quality Inventory, Section 305b Report. Water Quality Management Division, Non point Source Unit. Baton Rouge, LA.

Louisiana Geologic Survey. 1990. Generalized geology of Louisiana. Information obtained from the website http://www.lgs.lsu.edu/lgs/gengeo.html.

Low, J.B., and F.C. Bellrose, Jr. 1944. The seed and vegetative yield of waterfowl food plants in the Illinois River Valley. Journal of Wildlife Management 8:7-22.

Lower Mississippi Region Comprehensive Study Coordinating Committee. 1974. Lower Mississippi Region Comprehensive Study. Appendix Q, Fish and Wildlife. 143 pp.

Marie, J.R. 1971. Ground-water resources of Avoyelles Parish, Louisiana. USGS Water Resources Bulletin No. 15. 70 pp.

Martin, P.G. 1986. Soil Survey of Avoyelles Parish, Louisiana. U.S. Department of Agriculture, Soil Conservation Service. 162 p.

McGilvrey, F.B. 1968. A guide to Wood Duck production habitat requirements. U.S. Fish and Wildlife Service. Research Publication 60. 32 pp.

Mitsch, W.J. and J.G. Gosselink. 1993. Wetlands. Second Edition. Van Nostrand Reinhold, New York, New York. 722 pp.

Moore, L. 1993. Population dynamics and habitat requirements of wild turkeys in the Quachita Mountain range. Annual Progress Report, University of Arkansas Cooperative Wildlife and Fish Unit, Fayetteville, Arkansas. 4pp.

Mueller, A. J., D.J. Twedt, and C.R. Loesch. Development of Management Objectives for breeding birds in the Mississippi Alluvial Valley in R. Bonney, D. N. Pashley, R. J. Cooper, and L. Niles, eds. 1999. Strategies for Bird Conservation: The Partners in Flight Planning Process. Cornell Lab of Ornithology.

Neuman, Robert W . 1984, . An Introduction to Louisiana Archaeology, Baton Rouge, Louisiana State Press.

Reincke, K.J. and C.K. Baxter. 1996. Waterfowl Habitat Management in the Mississippi Alluvial Valley. Pages 159-167 in J.T. Ratti, Editor. 7th International Waterfowl Symposium.

Reinecke, K.J., and C.R. Loesch. 1996. Integrating research and management to conserve wildfowl (Anatidae) and wetlands in the Mississippi Alluvial Valley, U.S.A. Gibier Faune Sauvage, Game and Wildlife 13:927-940.

Reinecke, K.J., Kaminski, R.M., Moorhead, D.J., Hodges, J.D., and Nassar, J.R. 1989. Mississippi Alluvial Valley. in Habitat management for migrating and wintering waterfowl in North America edited by Smith, L.M., Pederson, R.L. and Kaminski, R.M. 1989. Texas Tech University Press. 560pp.

Saucier, C.L. 1943. History of Avoyelles Parish, Louisiana. New Orleans, LA: Pelican Publishing Company.

Saucier, R.T. 1994. Geomorphology and Quaternary Geologic History of the Lower Mississippi Valley (2 volumes). U.S. Army Engineer Waterways Experiment Station, Vicksburg, Mississippi.

Scott, C.D. 1973. Seasonal food habitats of the European wild hog in the Great Smoky Mountains National Park. M.S. Thesis, Univ. Tenn., 54pp.

Shea D., C.S. Hofeltet, D.R. Luellen, A. Huysman, P.R. Lazaro, R. Zarzecki, and J.R. Kelly. 2001. Chemical contamination at National Wildlife Refuges in the Lower Mississippi River Ecosystem. Report by NC State University to the US Fish and Wildlife Service, Atlanta, GA. 40pp.

St. Amant, L.S. 1959. Louisiana Wildlife Inventory and Management Plan. Pittman-Robertson Section, Fish and Game Division. Louisiana Wildlife and Fisheries Commission.

Teskey, R.O., and T.M. Hinckley. 1977. Impact of water level changes on woody riparian and wetland communities. Vol. II: Southern Forest Region. USFWS, Biological Services Program. FWS/OBS-77/59. 46 pp.

Toth, Edwin A. 1974 *Archaeology and Ceramics of the Marksville Site*. Anthropological Papers No. 56, Museum of Anthropology, University of Michigan, Ann Arbor.

University of New Orleans, Division of Business and Economic Research. 1999. Revenues, Payroll, and Employment Generated By Tourism, Louisiana and Parishes:. New Orleans, LA: University Orleans.

U.S. Army Corps of Engineers. 1975. Environmental assessment for eastern Rapides and south central Avoyelles Parishes Project. New Orleans District, LA. Chapter II, pp. 2-5.

U.S. Department of Agriculture, Forest Service. 1991. Forest Statistics for Louisiana Parishes - 1991. Washington, D.C.: U.S. Government Printing Office.

U.S. Department of Commerce, Bureau of the Census. 1980. Statistics of the Population of the United States in 1980. Twentieth Census. Washington, D.C.: U.S. Government Printing Office.

U.S. Department of Commerce, Bureau of the Census. 1990. Statistics of the Population of the United States in 1990. Twentieth-first Census. Washington, D.C.: U.S. Government Printing Office.

U.S. Department of Commerce, Bureau of the Census. 1996. U.S.A. Counties 1996,General Profile, Avoyelles, LA. Washington, D.C.:U.S. Government Printing Office

U.S. Department of Commerce, Bureau of the Census. 1993. County Business Patterns, Avoyelles Parish, LA. Washington, D.C.:U.S. Government Printing Office.

U.S. Department of Commerce, Bureau of the Census. 1996. County Business Patterns, Avoyelles Parish, LA. Washington, D.C.: U.S. Government Printing Office.

U.S. Department of Commerce, Bureau of the Census, Small Area Income and Poverty Estimates Program. 1999. Model-Based Income and Poverty Estimates for Avoyelles Parish. Washington, D.C.: U.S. Government Printing Office.

U.S. Department of Commerce. 1992. Census of Agriculture, Louisiana, 1992. Washington, D.C.: U.S. Department of Agriculture.

U.S. Fish and Wildlife Service. 1979. A supplemental report on the eastern Rapides, south-central Avoyelles Parishes, Louisiana, Project. Lafayette, LA. 23 pp.

U.S. Fish and Wildlife Service. 1979. Below Red River levee project, Red River backwater area, Louisiana. Fish and Wildlife Coordination Act Report. Vicksburg, MS.

U.S. Fish and Wildlife Service. 1989. Purchase of lands for the establishment of Lake Ophelia National Wildlife Refuge, Avoyelles Parish, Louisiana. Final Environmental Assessment. Atlanta, GA.

U.S. Fish and Wildlife Service, Southeast Region. 1989. Approval Memorandum for the Purchase of Lands for the Establishment of Lake Ophelia National Wildlife Refuge, Avoyelles Parish, Louisiana.

U.S. Fish and Wildlife Service. 1996. National Survey of Fishing, Hunting and Wildlife Associated Recreation.

U.S. Fish and Wildlife Service. 1998. Lake Ophelia and Grand Cote Refuge Complex Biological Update/Recommendations. Atlanta, GA

U.S Fish and Wildlife Service. 1990. American Woodcock management Plan. 11 pp.

U.S Fish and Wildlife Service. 2005. Lake Ophelia National Wildlife Refuge Comprehensive Conservation Plan. 160 pp.

Vermillion, W. G. and D. A. Walther. 2001. Spring Bayou, Louisiana Reconnaissance Study: A Planning-Aid Report. U.S. Fish and Wildlife Service. 34pp.

Wiley, A.G. 1987. Feral hog management at Golden Gate National Recreation Area; Proc. Calif. Confer. Conserv. Manage. 189-191.

Wilson et al. 2000. Mississippi Alluvial Valley Shorebird Conservation Plan.

Yarrow, G.K. 1987. The potential for interspecific resource competition between white-tailed deer and feral hogs in the post oak savannah region of Texas. M.S. Thesis. Stephen R. Austin State University. 222pp.

Appendix III. Relevant Legal Mandates

National Wildlife Refuge System Authorities

The mission of the Fish and Wildlife Service is to conserve, protect, and enhance the nation's fish and wildlife and their habitats for the continuing benefit of the American people. The Service is the primary Federal agency responsible for migratory birds, endangered plants and animals, certain marine mammals, and anadromous fish. This responsibility to conserve our nation's fish and wildlife resources is shared with other Federal agencies and State and tribal governments.

As part of this responsibility, the Service manages the National Wildlife Refuge System. This system is the only nationwide system of federal land managed and protected for wildlife and their habitats. The mission of the National Wildlife Refuge System is to administer a national network of lands and waters for the conservation, management, and, where appropriate, restoration of the fish, wildlife, and plant resources and their habitats within the United States for the benefit of present and future generations of Americans.

Grand Cote National Wildlife Refuge is managed as part of this system in accordance with the National Wildlife Refuge System Administration Act of 1966, as amended by the National Wildlife Refuge System Improvement Act of 1997, the Refuge Recreation Act of 1962, Executive Order 12996 (Management and General Public Use of the National Wildlife Refuge System), Biological Integrity, Diversity, and Environmental Health Policy, and other relevant legislation, executive orders, regulations, and policies.

Key Legislation/Policies for Plan Implementation

The Grand Cote National Wildlife Refuge Comprehensive Conservation Plan describes and illustrates management-area projects with standards and guidelines for future decision-making and may be adjusted through monitoring and evaluation, as well as amendment and revision. The plan approval establishes conservation and land protection goals, objectives, and specific strategies for the refuge and its expansion. Compatible recreation uses specific to the refuge have been identified and approved by the refuge manager. This plan provides for systematic stepping down from the overall direction as outlined when making project- or activity-level decisions. This level involves site-specific analysis (e.g., Forest Habitat Management Plan) to meet National Environmental Policy Act requirements for decision-making.

The legal mandates supporting the National Wildlife Refuge System are as follows:

Antiquities Act (1906): Authorizes the scientific investigation of antiquities on Federal land and provides penalties for unauthorized removal of objects taken or collected without a permit.

Migratory Bird Treaty Act (1918): Designates the protection of migratory birds as a Federal responsibility. This act enables the setting of seasons, and other regulations including the closing of areas, federal or non-federal, to the hunting of migratory birds.

Migratory Bird Conservation Act (1929): Establishes procedures for acquisition by purchase, rental, or gift of areas approved by the Migratory Bird Conservation Commission.

Fish and Wildlife Act (1956): Established a comprehensive national fish and wildlife policy and broadened the authority for acquisition and development of refuges.

Fish and Wildlife Coordination Act (1958): Allows the Fish and Wildlife Service to enter into agreements with private landowners for wildlife management purposes.

Refuge Recreation Act (1962): Allows the use of refuges for recreation when such uses are compatible with the refuge's primary purposes and when sufficient funds are available to manage the uses.

Land and Water Conservation Fund Act (1965): Uses the receipts from the sale of surplus Federal land, outer continental shelf oil and gas sales, and other sources for land acquisition under several authorities.

Architectural Barriers Act (1968): Requires federally owned, leased, or funded buildings and facilities to be accessible to persons with disabilities.

National Environmental Policy Act (1969): Requires the disclosure of the environmental impacts of any major Federal action significantly affecting the quality of the human environment.

Rehabilitation Act (1973): Requires that programmatic and physical accessibility be made available in any facility funded by the Federal Government, ensuring that anyone can participate in any program.

Americans with Disabilities Act (1992): Prohibits discrimination in public accommodations and services.

Clean Water Act (1977): Requires consultation with the U.S. Army Corps of Engineers for major wetland modifications.

Executive Order 11988 (1977): Requires every Federal agency to provide leadership and take action to reduce the risk of flood loss and minimize the impact of floods on human safety, and to preserve the natural and beneficial values served by the floodplain.

Executive Order 11990: Directs Federal agencies to (1) minimize destruction, loss, or degradation of wetlands and (2) preserve and enhance the natural and beneficial values of wetlands when a practical alternative exists.

Emergency Wetlands Resources Act (1986): The purpose of the act is "To promote the conservation of migratory waterfowl and to offset or prevent the serious loss of wetlands by the acquisition of wetlands and other essential habitat, and for other purposes."

Federal Noxious Weed Act (1990): Requires the use of integrated management systems to control or contain undesirable plant species; requires an interdisciplinary approach with the cooperation of other Federal and State agencies.

Executive Order 12996, Management and General Public Use of the National Wildlife Refuge System (1996): Defines the mission, purpose, and priority public uses of the National Wildlife Refuge System. It also presents four principles to guide management of the Refuge System.

Executive Order 13007, Indian Sacred Sites (1996): Directs Federal land management agencies to accommodate access to and ceremonial use of Indian sacred sites by Indian religious practitioners, avoid adversely affecting the physical integrity of such sacred sites, and where appropriate, maintain the confidentiality of sacred sites.

Emergency Wetland Resources Act of 1986: This act authorized the purchase of wetlands from Land and Water Conservation Fund moneys, removing a prior prohibition on such acquisitions. The act also requires the Secretary of the Interior to establish a National Wetlands Priority Conservation Plan, requires the states to include wetlands in their Comprehensive Outdoor Recreation Plans, and transfers to the Migratory Bird Conservation Fund an amount equal to import duties on arms and ammunition.

Endangered Species Act of 1973 (16 U.S.C. 1531-1544, 87 Stat. 884), as amended: Public Law 93-205, approved December 28, 1973, repealed the Endangered Species Conservation Act of December 5, 1969 (P.L. 91-135, 83 Stat. 275). The 1969 act amended the Endangered Species Preservation Act of October 15, 1966 (P.L. 89-669, 80 Stat. 926). The 1973 Endangered Species Act provided for the conservation of ecosystems upon which threatened and endangered species of fish, wildlife, and plants depend, both through Federal action and by encouraging the establishment of State programs. The act authorizes the determination and listing of species as threatened and endangered; prohibits unauthorized taking, possession, sale, and transport of endangered species; provides authority to acquire land for the conservation of listed species, using land and water conservation funds; authorizes establishment of cooperative agreements and grants-in-aid to States that establish and maintain active and adequate programs for threatened and endangered wildlife and plants; authorizes the assessment of civil and criminal penalties for violating the act or regulations that implement it; and authorizes the payment of rewards to anyone furnishing information leading to arrest and conviction of anyone violating the act and any regulation issued thereunder.

Environmental Education Act of 1990 (20 USC 5501-5510; 104 Stat. 3325): Public Law 101-619, signed November 16,1990, established the Office of Environmental Education within the Environmental Protection Agency to develop and administer a Federal environmental education program. Responsibilities of the office include developing and supporting programs to improve understanding of the natural and developed environment, and the relationships between humans and their environment; supporting the dissemination of educational materials; developing and supporting training programs and environmental education seminars; managing a Federal grant program; and administering an environmental internship and fellowship program. The Office is required to develop and support environmental programs in consultation with other Federal natural resource management agencies, including the Fish and Wildlife Service.

Executive Order 11988, Floodplain Management: The purpose of this executive order, signed May 24, 1977, is to prevent Federal agencies from contributing to the "adverse impacts associated with occupancy and modification of floodplains" and the "direct or indirect support of floodplain development." In the course of fulfilling their respective authorities, Federal agencies "shall take action to reduce the risk of flood loss, to minimize the impact of floods on human safety, health and welfare, and to restore and preserve the natural and beneficial values served by flood plains."

Fish and Wildlife Improvement Act of 1978: This act was passed to improve the administration of fish and wildlife programs; it and amends several earlier laws, including the Refuge Recreation Act, the National Wildlife Refuge System Administration Act, and the Fish and Wildlife Act of 1956. It authorizes the Secretary of the Interior to accept gifts and bequests of real and personal property on behalf of the United States. It also authorizes the use of volunteers on Service projects and appropriations to carry out volunteer programs.

Historic Preservation Acts include:

- Archaeological Resources Protection Act (16 U.S.C. 470aa - 47011) -- Public Law 96-95, approved October 31, 1979, (93 Stat. 721) largely supplanted the resource protection provisions of the Antiquities Act for archaeological items. This act established detailed requirements for issuance of permits for any excavation for or removal of archaeological resources from Federal and Indian lands. It also established civil and criminal penalties for the unauthorized excavation, removal, or damage of any such resources; for any trafficking in such resources removed from federal and Indian lands in violation of any provision of federal law; and for interstate and foreign commerce in such resources acquired, transported, or received in violation of any State or local law.

- Public Law 100-588, approved November 3, 1988, (102 Stat. 2983) lowered the threshold value of artifacts triggering the felony provisions of the act from $5,000 to $500, made attempting to commit an action prohibited by the act a violation, and required the land-managing agencies to establish public awareness programs regarding the value of archaeological resources to the nation.

- Archaeological and Historic Preservation Act (16 U.S.C. 469-469c)--Public Law 86-523, approved June 27, 1960 (74 Stat. 220), and amended by Public Law 93-291, approved May 24, 1974 (88 Stat. 174), directed Federal agencies to notify the Secretary of the Interior whenever a Federal, federally assisted, or licensed or permitted project may cause loss or destruction of significant scientific, prehistoric, or archaeological data. The act authorized use of appropriated, donated, and/or transferred funds for the recovery, protection, and preservation of such data.

- Historic Sites, Buildings, and Antiquities Act (16 U.S.C. 461-462, 464-467)--The act of August 21,1935 (49 Stat. 666), popularly known as the Historic Sites Act, as amended by Public Law 89-249, approved October 9,1965, (79 Stat. 971), declared it a national policy to preserve historic sites and objects of national significance, including those located on Refuges. It provided procedures for designation, acquisition, administration, and protection of such sites. Among other things, National Historic and Natural Landmarks are designated under authority of this act. As of January, 1989, thirty-one national wildlife Refuges contained such sites.

- National Historic Preservation Act of 1966 (16 U.S.C. 470-470b, 470c-470n)--Public Law 89-665, approved October 15, 1966, (80 Stat. 915) and repeatedly amended, provided for preservation of significant historical features (buildings, objects, and sites) through a grant-in-aid program to the states. It established a National Register of Historic Places and a program of matching grants under the existing National Trust for Historic Preservation (16 U.S.C. 468-468d).

- The act established an Advisory Council on Historic Preservation, which was made a permanent independent agency in Public Law 94-422, approved September 28, 1976 (90 Stat. 1319). That act also created the Historic Preservation Fund. Federal agencies are directed to take into account the effects of their actions on items or sites listed in, or eligible for listing in, the National Register of Historic Places. As of January 1989, ninety-one such sites on national wildlife refuges are listed in this register.

Land and Water Conservation Fund Act of 1948: This act provides funding through receipts from the sale of surplus Federal land, appropriations from oil and gas receipts from the outer continental shelf, and other sources of land acquisition under several authorities. Appropriations from the fund may be used for matching grants to states for outdoor recreation projects and for land acquisition by various Federal agencies, including the Fish and Wildlife Service.

Migratory Bird Hunting and Conservation Stamp Act (16 U.S.C. 718-718j, 48 Stat. 452), as amended: The "Duck Stamp Act," of March 16,1934, authorizes the opening of part of a refuge to waterfowl hunting and requires each waterfowl hunter 16 years of age or older to possess a valid Federal hunting stamp. Receipts from the sale of the stamp are deposited in a special Treasury account known as the Migratory Bird Conservation Fund and are not subject to appropriations.

National and Community Service Act of 1960 (42 U.S.C. 12401:104 Stat. 3127), Public Law 101-610, signed November 16,1990, authorizes several programs to engage citizens of the United States in full- and/or part-time projects designed to combat illiteracy and poverty, provide job skills, enhance educational skills, and fulfill environmental needs. Several provisions are of particular interest to the Fish and Wildlife Service.

Native American Graves Protection and Repatriation Act (1990): Requires Federal agencies and museums to inventory, determine ownership of, and repatriate cultural items under their control or possession.

American Conservation and Youth Service Corps: A Federal grant program established under Subtitle C of the law, the Corps offers an opportunity for young adults between the ages of 16-25, or in the case of summer programs, 15-21, to engage in approved human and natural resources projects which benefit the public or are carried out on federal or Indian lands. To be eligible for assistance, natural resource programs must focus on improvement of wildlife habitat and recreational areas, fish culture, fishery assistance, erosion, wetlands protection, pollution control, and similar projects. A stipend of not more than 100 percent of the poverty level will be paid to participants. A Commission established to administer the Youth Service Corps will make grants to States, the Secretaries of Agriculture and Interior, and the Director of ACTION to carry out these responsibilities.

National Environmental Policy Act of 1959 (P.L. 91-190,42 U.S.C. 4321-4347, January 1, 1970, 83 Stat. 852) as amended by Public Law 94-52, July 3, 1975, 89 Stat. 258, and Public Law 94-83, August 9,1975, 89 Stat. 424). Title I of the 1969 National Environmental Policy Act requires that all Federal agencies prepare detailed environmental impact statements for "every recommendation or report on proposals for legislation and other major federal actions significantly affecting the quality of the human environment." The 1969 statute stipulated the factors to be considered in environmental impact statements, and required that Federal agencies employ an interdisciplinary approach in related decision making and develop means to ensure that unquantified environmental values are given appropriate consideration, along with economic and technical considerations. Title II of this statute requires annual reports on environmental quality from the President to the Congress, and established a Council on Environmental Quality in the Executive Office of the President with specific duties and functions.

National Wildlife Refuge System Improvement Act of 1997 (Refuge Administration Act), Public Law 105-57, amends the National Wildlife Refuge System Act of 1966 (16 U.S.C. 668dd-ee) and provides guidance for management and public use of the Refuge System. The act defines the National Wildlife Refuge System and authorizes the Secretary of the Interior to permit any use of a refuge provided such use is compatible with the major purposes for which the refuge was established. It mandates that the Refuge System be consistently directed and managed as a national system of lands and waters devoted to wildlife conservation and management. The Refuge Improvement Act clearly defines a unifying mission for the Refuge System. It establishes the legitimacy and appropriateness of the six priority public uses (hunting, fishing, wildlife observation, wildlife photography, and environmental education and interpretation); these activities are to be promoted on the Refuge System, while all non-wildlife-dependent uses are subject to compatibility determinations. The act establishes a formal process for determining compatibility; a compatible use is one which, in the sound professional judgment of the Refuge Manger, will not materially interfere with, or detract from, fulfillment of the National Wildlife Refuge System Mission or Refuge purpose(s). The act establishes the responsibilities of the Secretary of the Interior for managing and protecting the Refuge System; and requires a Comprehensive Conservation Plan for each Refuge by the year 2012. As stated in the act, "The mission of the system is to administer a national network of lands and waters for the conservation, management, and where appropriate, restoration of the fish, wildlife, and plant resources and their habitats within the United States for the benefit of present and future generations of Americans." The act also requires development of a comprehensive conservation plan for each refuge and that management is consistent with the plan. When writing a plan for expanded or new refuges, and when making management decisions, the act requires effective coordination with other Federal agencies, State fish and wildlife or conservation agencies, and refuge neighbors. A refuge must also provide opportunities for public involvement when making a compatibility determination.

North American Wetlands Conservation Act (103 Stat. 1968; 16 U.S.C. 4401-4412) Public Law 101-233, enacted December 13, 1989, provides funding and administrative direction for implementation of the North American Waterfowl Management Plan and the Tripartite Agreement on Wetlands between Canada, the United States, and Mexico. The act converts the Pittman-Robertson account into a trust fund, with the interest available without appropriation through the year 2006, to carry out the programs authorized by the act, along with an authorization for annual appropriation of $15 million plus an amount equal to the fines and forfeitures collected under the Migratory Bird Treaty Act. Available funds may be expended, upon approval of the Migratory Bird Conservation Commission, for payment not to exceed 50 percent of the United States' share of the cost of wetlands conservation projects in Canada, Mexico, or the United States (or 100 percent of the cost of projects on Federal lands). At least 50 percent and no more than 70 percent of the funds received are to go to Canada and Mexico each year.

Refuge Recreation Act of 1952: This act authorizes the Secretary of the Interior to administer refuges, hatcheries, and other conservation areas for recreational use, when such uses do not interfere with the area's primary purposes. It authorizes construction and maintenance of recreational facilities and acquisition of land for incidental fish- and wildlife-dependent recreational development or protection of natural resources. It also authorizes the charging of fees for public uses.

Refuge Revenue Sharing Act (16 U.S.C. 715s) Section 401 of the act of June 15,1935, (49 Stat. 383) provided for payments to counties in lieu of taxes, using revenues derived from the sale of products from Refuges. Public Law 88-523, approved August 30,1964, (78 Stat. 701) made major revisions to the Refuge Revenue Sharing Act by requiring that all revenues received from refuge products, such as animals, timber and minerals, or from leases or other privileges, be deposited in a special Treasury account and net receipts distributed to counties for public schools and roads. Public Law 93-509, approved December 3, 1974, (88 Stat. 1603) required that moneys remaining in the fund after payment be transferred to the Migratory Bird Conservation Fund for land acquisition under provisions of the Migratory Bird Conservation Act. Public Law 95-469, approved October 17, 1978, (92 Stat. 1319) expanded the revenue-sharing system to include national fish hatcheries and Service research stations. It also included in the Refuge Revenue Sharing Fund receipts from the sale of salmonid carcasses. Payments to counties were established as follows: on acquired land, the greatest amount calculated on the basis of 75 cents per acre, three-fourths of one percent of the appraised value, or 25 percent of the net receipts produced from the land; and on land withdrawn from the public domain, 25 percent of net receipts and basic payments under Public Law 94-565 (31 U.S.C. 1601-1607, 90 Stat. 2662). This amendment also authorized appropriations to make up any difference between the amount in the fund and the amount scheduled for payment in any year. The stipulation that payments be used for schools and roads was removed, but counties were required to pass payments along to other units of local government within the county which suffer losses in revenues due to the establishment of Service areas.

Wilderness Act of 1954: Public Law 88-577, approved September 3, 1964, directed the Secretary of the Interior, within 10 years, to review every roadless area of 5,000 or more acres and every roadless island (regardless of size) within National Wildlife Refuge and National Park Systems for inclusion in the National Wilderness Preservation System.

Appendix IV. Public Involvement

PUBLIC INVOLVEMENT PROCESS

Public involvement in the development of the Draft Comprehensive Conservation Plan and Environment Assessment for Grand Cote National Wildlife Refuge, in Avoyelles Parish, Louisiana, was sought throughout the planning process. A planning team (refer to Section B, Appendix VIII) composed of representatives from various Service divisions was formed to prepare the Draft Plan and Environmental Assessment. Initially, the team focused on identifying the issues and concerns pertinent to refuge management. The team met on several occasions from February 2004 to August 2005.

In preparation for developing the Draft Plan, a Wildlife and Habitat (Biological) Review was conducted on Grand Cote Refuge during the week of October 20-22, 2003, by a team of Service biologists, managers, foresters, and non-service managers/biologists (refer to Section B, Chapter V). A final report for the Biological Review was completed in February 2004. A Visitor Service Review Report was completed in November 2003. A notice of intent was published on February 19, 2004 (69 FR 7790), to officially inform the public of the preparation of the comprehensive conservation plan for Grand Cote Refuge. To expand the range of issues and generate potential alternatives, public input to the development of the Draft Plan was sought through two public scoping meetings held on March 9 and 11, 2004, at Marksville and Bunkie High Schools, Avoyelles Parish, Louisiana. At the meetings, interested stakeholders were able to register their concerns to ensure that they would be considered in developing the Draft Plan. The meetings were publicized by a press release in the local papers in Alexandria, Marksville, Ville Platte, Jena, Bunkie, and Lafayette, Louisiana, and were broadcasted on two local radio stations. There were 19 attendees at the meetings, and several meeting attendees provided public comment. One citizen sent a comment letter to the refuge.

The issues generated from these public scoping meetings, coupled with the input of the planning team, are summarized in Section A, Chapter III. Over a 2-year period, a plan was developed for the refuge, which will serve as a management guide over the next 15 years.

Approximately 110 copies of the draft plan were made available for public review, beginning June 16, 2006, and ending July 31, 2006. Individuals reviewing this document represented landowners, conservation organizations, and state and local government agencies. A flyer which announced the dates of the comment period, and the date and location of the public meeting to discuss the draft, was mailed along with the plans. A public meeting was held on July 6, 2006 at 6:30 p.m., at the Marksville Fire Station, Marksville, Louisiana. Twenty-eight individuals were in attendance at the meeting. Seven individuals presented oral comments and eight respondents submitted written comments either by phone, mail, or email. Draft plan comments and the Service response to those comments are summarized below.

DRAFT PLAN COMMENTS AND SERVICE RESPONSE

General

There was one comment that questioned the refuge's proposed management action and suggested that Alternative 3 be adopted. One comment supported the proposed action and had no objection to the plan. The Service believes that the selection of Alternative 2 as the proposed action best meets the purpose and goals of the refuge.

One respondent provided general editorial comments as well as updated information to include in the hydrology restoration sections of the plan. The Service will incorporate these changes and update the information.

Fish and Wildlife Population Management

One comment was received regarding wood duck productivity on the refuge. The respondent expressed concern that the refuge was not fulfilling one of the main purposes by not providing better nesting and brood habitat and was disappointed that refuge staff could not accomplish this objective. The Service realized there was an error in the draft plan on page 46 that stated "Due to other priorities the limited number of boxes on the refuge has not been maintained and nest success is presumed to be low." Since the Biological Review in 2003, the refuge has increased and improved nesting and brood habitat on the refuge. The wood duck nest box program has expanded and over 140 nest boxes are maintained and nest success is monitored. Brood habitat has improved through better water management and restoration. Upon implementation of the plan, the Service intends to continue to improve the productivity of wood ducks on the refuge by increasing the wood duck nest box program and providing more high quality brood habitat. The Service will also continue to meet and exceed wood duck banding goals. The Service has corrected this portion of the plan to better reflect the information provided above.

Habitat Management

One respondent expressed concern over the lack of any reforestation on the refuge and believes the refuge should be restored to the original bottomland hardwood forest habitat type. The respondent states that given the 75 percent reduction of bottomland hardwood forests in this area, ecosystem alterations, global warming concerns, and the continued clearing of forest by private landowners, restoration of this habitat type on public lands is warranted. The Service selected Alternative 2, which promotes a diversity of habitats instead of reforesting the entire refuge (Alternative 3 – Restoration of the endemic ecosystem) in order to best meet the refuge purposes. The Service agrees that the reduction of bottomland hardwood forests in the Mississippi Alluvial Valley is alarming; however, Grand Cote Refuge is not part of the national plan for forest breeding birds or Louisiana black bear, which target reforestation of bottomland hardwood forests. In fact, the refuge is not part of the national plans because the area would act as a habitat sink, attracting many sensitive species to an area that does not meet the habitat requirements and has increased amounts of edge. This, in turn, will ultimately decrease production of these species and increase productivity of pest/invasive species, such as brown-headed cowbirds.

Resource Protection

Many comments were received regarding resource protection. Four respondents requested the refuge participate in the Avoyelles Parish Flood Hazard Mitigation Plan (Kisatchie-Delta Regional Planning and Development District, Inc., 2003). The comments specifically requested that the refuge incorporate hydrology restoration efforts suggested in the Mitigation Plan, such as breeching levees, which would allow water onto the refuge and deposit sediment, in order to help restore Spring Bayou and alleviate flood problems in Avoyelles Parish. One respondent stated that the Corps is conducting a feasibility study and will evaluate a number of alternatives to restore hydrology to the Spring Bayou WMA and this could include providing additional water to Grand Cote and Lake Ophelia Refuges, which could be included within the Corps' evaluation. The Service supports this landscape level watershed management endeavor and will participate as appropriate. Goal C, Objective C-3 in the plan outlines the Service's intent to participate in this endeavor. The Service believes a complete hydrological and water quality assessment will need to be completed in conjunction with this endeavor. The Service would like to coordinate with the Army Corp of Engineers, the Avoyelles Parish Police Jury, Avoyelles Wildlife Federation, and other interested partners on the Avoyelles Parish Flood Hazard Mitigation Plan and Spring Bayou Restoration Plan, and ensure that opportunities for fish and wildlife habitat are enhanced and do not materially detract from the purposes of the refuge.

Two comments were received regarding land protection within the refuge acquisition boundary. One respondent wanted to know if there would be money available to purchase additional land in the Chatlain Lake Unit Acquisition area. Another respondent suggested the refuge secure funds to take care of lands that it owns before acquiring more land.   The plan outlines goals, objectives, and strategies to protect inholdings and 2,500-3,000 acres in the Chatlain Lake Unit to better meet waterfowl and shorebird objectives. The plan also outlines objectives and strategies to provide better resource protection and management of lands within current ownership.

Visitor Services

One respondent would like to limit the refuge to archery deer hunting only while another comment was to increase access, deer hunting, and duck hunting. One respondent wondered why Grand Cote Refuge's deer season coincided with the State season and Lake Ophelia Refuge's season differed. Two respondents would also like the refuge to provide more environmental education programs and allow more public use. One respondent would like the refuge to allow horseback riding weekends on designated areas from April 1st to September 30th to avoid the hunting season. The respondent suggested that checkout time would be 8 p.m. and could involve a fee. The refuge will try to balance the needs of different user groups, recognizing that all needs may not be met; however, the plan outlines increases in wildlife-dependent recreational activities, including environmental education and interpretation, wildlife observation, and wildlife photography. These comments concerning visitor services will be addressed in specific step-down management plans that need to be either developed or updated.

Appendix V. Compatibility Determination

Uses: The following uses were considered for compatibility determination reviews: 1) hunting; 2) fishing; 3) wildlife observation and photography; 4) environmental education and interpretation 5) all-terrain vehicle use; 6) cooperative farming program; and 7) refuge resource research studies. A description and anticipated biological impacts for each use are addressed separately in this compatibility determination.

Refuge Name: Grand Cote National Wildlife Refuge

Date Established: March 17, 1989

Establishing and Acquisition Authority: The refuge was established in 1989 under the authority of the Fish and Wildlife Act of 1956 which calls for:

"...for the development, advancement, management, conservation, and protection of fish and wildlife resources..." [16 USC 742f(a)(4)];

the Emergency Wetlands Resources Act of 1986, which calls for:
"...the conservation of the wetlands of the Nation in order to maintain the public benefits they provide and to help fulfill international obligations contained in various migratory bird treaties and conventions..." (16 USC 3901 (b), 100 Stat. 3583);

and the Migratory Bird Conservation Act as amended in 1989, which calls for:
"... use as an inviolate sanctuary, or any other management purpose, for migratory birds," (USC 715d).

Refuge Purposes: The purposes for which Grand Cote Refuge was established are:

- Conserve wintering habitat for mallards, pintails, blue-winged teal, and wood ducks and production habitat for wood ducks to meet the goals of the North American Waterfowl Management Plan.

- Provide habitat and protection for endangered and threatened species.

- Provide habitat for a natural diversity of wildlife and plant species.

- Provide opportunities for wildlife-dependent recreation and environmental education when compatible with other refuge objectives.

National Wildlife Refuge System Mission:

The mission of the Refuge System, as defined by the National Wildlife Refuge System Improvement Act of 1997, is:

... to administer a national network of lands and waters for the conservation, management, and where appropriate, restoration of the fish, wildlife and plant resources and their habitats within the United States for the benefit of present and future generations of Americans.

Other Applicable Laws, Regulations, and Policies:

Antiquities Act of 1906 (34 Stat. 225)
Migratory Bird Treaty Act of 1918 (15 U.S.C. 703-711; 40 Stat. 755)
Migratory Bird Conservation Act of 1929 (16 U.S.C. 715r; 45 Stat. 1222)
Migratory Bird Hunting Stamp Act of 1934 (16 U.S.C. 718-178h; 48 Stat. 451)
Criminal Code Provisions of 1940 (18 U.S.C. 41)
Bald and Golden Eagle Protection Act (16 U.S.C. 668-668d; 54 Stat. 250)
Refuge Trespass Act of June 25, 1948 (18 U.S.C. 41; 62 Stat. 686)
Fish and Wildlife Act of 1956 (16 U.S.C. 742a-742j; 70 Stat.1119)
Refuge Recreation Act of 1962 (16 U.S.C. 460k-460k-4; 76 Stat. 653)
Wilderness Act (16 U.S.C. 1131; 78 Stat. 890)
Land and Water Conservation Fund Act of 1965
National Historic Preservation Act of 1966, as amended (16 U.S.C. 470, et seq.; 80 Stat. 915)
National Wildlife Refuge System Administration Act of 1966 (16 U.S.C. 668dd, 668ee; 80 Stat. 927)
National Environmental Policy Act of 1969, NEPA (42 U.S.C. 4321, et seq; 83 Stat. 852)
Use of Off-Road Vehicles on Public Lands (Executive Order 11644, as amended by Executive Order 10989)
Endangered Species Act of 1973 (16 U.S.C. 1531 et seq; 87 Stat. 884)
Refuge Revenue Sharing Act of 1935, as amended in 1978 (16 U.S.C. 715s; 92 Stat. 1319)
National Wildlife Refuge Regulations for the Most Recent Fiscal Year (50 CFR Subchapter C; 43 CFR 3101.3-3)
Emergency Wetlands Resources Act of 1986 (S.B. 740)
North American Wetlands Conservation Act of 1990
Food Security Act (Farm Bill) of 1990 as amended (HR 2100)
The Property Clause of the U.S. Constitution Article IV 3, Clause 2
The Commerce Clause of the U.S. Constitution Article 1, Section 8
The National Wildlife Refuge System Improvement Act of 1997 (Public Law 105-57, USC668dd)
Executive Order 12996, Management and General Public Use of the National Wildlife Refuge System. March 25, 1996
Title 50, Code of Federal Regulations, Parts 25-33
Archaeological Resources Protection Act of 1979
Native American Graves Protection and Repatriation Act of 1990

Compatibility determinations for each description listed were considered separately. Although for brevity, the preceding sections from "Uses" through "Other Applicable Laws, Regulations and Policies" are only written once within the plan, they are part of each descriptive use and become part of that compatibility determination if considered outside of the comprehensive conservation plan.

Description of Use: Hunting

Grand Cote National Wildlife Refuge is a 6,075-acre refuge consisting of several different habitat types. Most of the refuge was, at one time, part of a vast bottomland hardwood forest, but was cleared in the 1970s for agriculture. A mix of reforested fields, agricultural fields, moist-soil management units, forested wetlands, sloughs, bayous, and canals make up the refuge. There are approximately 2,530 acres of agricultural fields and moist-soil units and 2,797 acres of bottomland hardwood forest and reforested or land reverting back to bottomland species. This mix provides good habitat for a number of game species, including white-tailed deer, rabbit, woodcock, and waterfowl.

Many of the local residents enjoy an informal, rural lifestyle that includes frequent recreational use of the area's natural resources. Hunting and fishing have been, and continue to be, popular uses of public lands. Hunting has been permitted on the refuge since 2004.

Recreational hunting occurs during state seasons, generally between October and February each year, and follows state regulations. There are additional refuge-specific regulations to supplement state regulations. These refuge-specific regulations are reviewed annually and will be incorporated into the refuge hunting brochure and permit that hunters are required to have before hunting on the refuge. There will be 2,197 acres open throughout the entire hunting season with an additional 1,552 acres open until November 1st.

The refuge was established to provide wintering habitat for mallards, pintails, blue-winged teal, and wood ducks; therefore, it is necessary to maintain existing waterfowl sanctuary areas. These sanctuary areas will be seasonally closed to all activities, but when appropriate, will be utilized as archery-only deer hunting areas until November 1st, as noted above.

Hunters will access the refuge via Little California Road out of Marksville and Highway 1194 out of Fifth Ward. All vehicular traffic is restricted to these two roads. Access into the refuge hunt areas will be via hiking, all-terrain vehicles, or non-motorized boat.

Availability of Resources: Enforcement of refuge regulations to protect trust resources and provide for a quality recreational opportunity will occur via regular patrols by refuge law enforcement officers. The headquarters is located on Grand Cote Refuge, so these patrols will be performed more frequently than on other more remote refuges in the Complex. Currently, the Complex has one full-time officer. Additionally, personnel from the Louisiana Department of Wildlife and Fisheries will patrol the refuge and assist officers when needed.

The hunt program at the refuge will cost approximately $25,000 annually, which includes costs to create and print the hunt brochure, provide law enforcement, and create and maintain parking areas and all-terrain vehicle trails. Participation in the hunt program is estimated to be between 500 and 1,000 visitors annually. The refuge is enrolled in the Recreational Fee Program and charges $15 for required hunt permits and a blind fee of $5 per hunter with a minimum of $10 blind. Eighty percent of this money will come back to the refuge to assist with the operation and management cost of having a hunt program.

Anticipated Impacts of the Use: Monitoring of harvest will be accomplished through daily self-clearing check in/out permits and data collection from refuge staff. This monitoring will provide a way to measure the health (population density relative to carrying capacity) of the impacted wildlife. If wildlife populations significantly change, that difference will be reflected in the harvest. The long-term impact of hunting will be monitored in the following way on a yearly basis.

Harvest management of big game (e.g., white-tailed deer) is the art of combining wildlife science and landowner objectives for the attainment of a specific management goal. Whenever possible, harvest management strategies should be based on objectives established as part of hunting plans developed for the area. The objective-setting process must be based on a complete analysis of biological data. Specific harvest objectives allow the setting of hunting regulations. Results of each hunting season will be thoroughly evaluated to ensure that the harvest management program remains dynamic and responsive to an evolving management environment (Bookhout 1994).

Harvest management of small game and furbearers (e.g., rabbit, raccoon, and beaver) is considerably different from that of both big game and migratory birds. Current literature suggests that user take (<50 percent of total mortality) of most upland game is compensatory; that factors, such as immigration from adjacent areas and density-dependent production, operate in most upland game populations; and that hunting usually does not significantly impact populations. Hunting is substituted for natural mortality. Production of large, annual surpluses of young allow for lengthy seasons and generous bag limits with little concern for over-harvest and minimal chance of population impacts in most areas (Bookhout 1994).

Harvest management of migratory birds (e.g., ducks and woodcock) is more difficult to assess. Migratory bird regulations are established at the federal level each year following a series of meetings involving both state and federal biologists. Harvest guidelines are based on population lengths, and framework dates (Bookhout 1994). Schmidt (1993) states, "In general, all studies have demonstrated a high degree of compensation of hunting mortality by other 'natural' mortality factors for harvest levels experienced to date." He also reports, "The proportion of waterfowl populations subject to hunting on refuges is very low, thus hunting is not likely to have an adverse impact on the status of any recognized waterfowl population in North America."

Based on available information, no threatened or endangered species, other than the bald eagle and Louisiana black bear, could potentially use the refuge. It is anticipated that the current levels and expected future levels of hunting or other wildlife-dependent recreation activities will not directly, indirectly, or cumulatively impact any listed, proposed, or candidate species or designated/proposed critical habitat. Data gathered from future biological surveys regarding the importance or potential importance of the refuge to threatened or endangered species or critical habitat (or proposed threatened, endangered, or critical habitat) could result in changes to public use activities across time; however, these changes should have no effect on listed species.

Incidental taking of other wildlife species, either illegally or unintentionally, may occur with any consumptive use program. At current and anticipated public use levels, incidental take will be very small and will not directly or cumulatively impact current or future populations of wildlife either on this refuge or in the surrounding areas. Implementation of an effective law enforcement program and development of site-specific refuge regulations/special conditions will eliminate most incidental take problems.

Public Review and Comment: This compatibility determination was part of the Draft Comprehensive Conservation Plan and Environmental Assessment for Grand Cote National Wildlife Refuge, which was announced in the Federal Register and made available for public comment from June 16 – July 31, 2006 (71 FR 34955). Methods used to solicit public review and comment included posted notices at the refuge headquarters and other locations; copies of the draft comprehensive conservation plan and environmental assessment distributed to adjacent landowners, the public, and local, state, and federal agencies; public meetings; news releases to area newspapers; and local radio announcements. The availability of the draft plan/environmental assessment, the comment period, and public meeting location were announced in the Alexandria Daily Town Talk on June 25, 2006, and in the Avoyelles Journal on July 2, 2006.

Determination (check one below):

       Use is Not Compatible
  __X__Use is Compatible with the Following Stipulations

Stipulations Necessary to Ensure Compatibility: Hunting will be permitted in accordance with the State of Louisiana regulations and licensing requirements. An environmental assessment is on file at the refuge headquarters as part of the Hunting Plan. The following stipulations will help ensure the refuge hunting program is compatible with refuge purposes:

- Time, date, and zone restrictions may vary in the future as refuge boundaries expand and public use demands change.
- Vehicles will be restricted to designated roads. All-terrain vehicles will be restricted to designated trails. Off-road travel will be limited to foot travel only.
- Firearms, bows, and other weapons will be prohibited except during designated hunting seasons.
- Hunting deer with dogs will not be allowed on the refuge. Use of dogs for hunting rabbit, waterfowl, and woodcock will be allowed during designated seasons only.
- Sanctuary areas will be maintained and seasonally closed to all uses.
- Camping overnight on the refuge will be prohibited.
- All hunts will be designed to provide quality user opportunities based upon known wildlife population levels and biological parameters. Hunt season dates and bag limits will be adjusted as needed to achieve balanced wildlife population levels within carrying capacities, regardless of impacts to user opportunities.
- As additional data is collected and a long-range hunt plan developed, additional refuge-specific regulations could be implemented. These regulations could include, but may not be limited to, season dates that differ from those in surrounding state zones, refuge permit requirements, and closed areas on a permanent or seasonal basis (to reduce disturbance to specific wildlife species or habitats, such as bird rookeries, wintering waterfowl or threatened/endangered species, or to provide for public safety).

Justification: Recreational hunting is one of the six priority public uses made available on national wildlife refuges as indicated by the National Wildlife Refuge System Improvement Act of 1997. This use will allow the visiting public to safely enjoy quality hunting on public land while non-hunting visitors enjoy wildlife observation and photography, hiking, or learning about the natural resources of the area.

Mandatory 15-year Re-evaluation Date: __11/17/2021__

Description of Use: Fishing

Permit sport fishing on Grand Cote Refuge for channel catfish, blue catfish, flathead catfish; and permit crawfishing. The refuge season will fall within the framework of the State of Louisiana season established by the Louisiana Department of Wildlife and Fisheries.

Availability of Resources: Enforcement of refuge regulations to protect trust resources and provide for a quality recreational opportunity will occur via regular patrols by refuge law enforcement officers. The headquarters is located on Grand Cote Refuge, so these patrols will be performed more frequently than on other more remote refuges in the Complex. Currently, the Complex has one full-time officer. Additionally, personnel from the Louisiana Department of Wildlife and Fisheries will patrol the refuge and assist officers when needed.

The fishing program at the refuge will cost approximately $25,000 annually, which includes costs to create and print the hunt brochure, provide law enforcement, and create and maintain parking areas and all-terrain vehicle trails. Participation in the fishing program is estimated to be between 500 and 1,000 visitors annually. The refuge is enrolled in the Recreational Fee Program and charges $15 for required fishing permits. Eighty percent of this money will come back to the refuge to assist with the operation and management cost of having a fishing program.

Anticipated Impacts of the Use: No adverse impacts are expected as a result of this use. Seasons will be established with the objective of preventing disturbance to migratory waterfowl.

Public Review and Comment: This compatibility determination was part of the Draft Comprehensive Conservation Plan and Environmental Assessment for Grand Cote National Wildlife Refuge, which was announced in the Federal Register and made available for public comment from June 16 – July 31, 2006 (71 FR 34955). Methods used to solicit public review and comment included posted notices at the refuge headquarters and other locations; copies of the draft comprehensive conservation plan and environmental assessment distributed to adjacent landowners, the public, and local, state, and federal agencies; public meetings; news releases to area newspapers; and local radio announcements. The availability of the draft plan/environmental assessment, the comment period, and public meeting location were announced in the Alexandria Daily Town Talk on June 25, 2006, and in the Avoyelles Journal on July 2, 2006.

Determination (check one below):

      Use is Not Compatible

  __X__ Use is Compatible with Following Stipulations

Stipulations Necessary to Ensure Compatibility: Sport fishing and crawfishing are permitted during daylight hours only. Boats and traps may not be left on the refuge overnight. Law enforcement efforts on the refuge will ensure compliance with State of Louisiana laws and refuge-specific regulations. All or parts of the refuge may be closed to fishing or crawfishing at any time if necessary for public safety, to provide wildlife sanctuary, or for administrative reasons.

Justification: Fishing is identified in the 1997 National Wildlife Refuge System Improvement Act as an activity that should be provided and expanded on refuges. Sport fishing and crawfishing will provide quality, wildlife-dependent recreation to the public and the opportunity to utilize a renewable resource. Providing this recreation is a refuge objective.

Mandatory 15-year Re-evaluation Date: __11/17/2021__

Description of Use: *Wildlife Observation and Photography*

Non-consumptive wildlife observation uses, such as birdwatching, auto tour routes, hiking, and nature photography, are minimal at this time due to the area's distance from large metropolitan areas and the general lack of access and facilities. It is estimated that 2,000 visits/year are attributed to wildlife observation and related activities.

It is anticipated that an increase in non-consumptive wildlife-dependent uses will occur over the next few years as facilities and access are provided and especially as the public and conservation groups become aware of the excellent birding/wildlife viewing opportunities on the refuge. This anticipated increase will develop as facilities are provided; a moderate number of users are expected.

There are 12 miles of refuge primary roads maintained for public vehicle travel. An additional 9 miles of refuge secondary roads are maintained for administrative purposes, while 17 miles of all-terrain vehicle trails for hunting and fishing access and 4 miles of foot trails are maintained for public use. Nine miles of all-terrain vehicle trails will be upgraded and converted to public vehicle travel, 12 miles of refuge primary roads will be upgraded to national refuge road standards and 4 miles of new foot trails will be created.

Availability of Resources: Based on a review of the refuge's budget allocated for this activity, there is adequate funding to ensure compatibility and to administer the use at its current level.

Anticipated Impacts of the Use: Wildlife observation and photography activities might result in some disturbance to wildlife, especially if visitors venture too close to one of the bird rookeries. Refuge road systems, foot trails, boardwalks, and wildlife observation platforms opened to public use will be located to minimize disturbance that could occur in these sensitive areas. If unacceptable levels of disturbance are identified at any time, sensitive sites will be closed to public entry. Some minimal trampling of vegetation also may occur.

Construction of foot trails, boardwalks, observation platforms, upgrading refuge roads, and converting all-terrain vehicle trails to vehicular traffic will alter small portions of the natural environment. Proper planning prior to construction, sediment retention, and grade stabilization features will reduce negative impacts to wetlands, threatened and endangered species, and species of special concern. Impacts such as trampling vegetation and wildlife disturbance by refuge visitors do occur, but is presently not significant. Upgrading refuge roads will reduce soil erosion associated with the current dirt roads and trails. Other potential negative impacts are caused by visitors violating refuge regulations, such as littering or illegally taking plants or wildlife. Refuge roads are maintained for habitat and biological management programs and law enforcement. Use of the roads by the public does incur added maintenance costs.

Public Review and Comment: This compatibility determination was part of the Draft Comprehensive Conservation Plan and Environmental Assessment for Grand Cote National Wildlife Refuge, which was announced in the Federal Register and made available for public comment from June 16 – July 31, 2006 (71 FR 34955). Methods used to solicit public review and comment included posted notices at the refuge headquarters and other locations; copies of the draft comprehensive conservation plan and environmental assessment distributed to adjacent landowners, the public, and local, state, and federal agencies; public meetings; news releases to area newspapers; and local radio announcements. The availability of the draft plan/environmental assessment, the comment period, and public meeting location were announced in the Alexandria Daily Town Talk on June 25, 2006, and in the Avoyelles Journal on July 2, 2006.

Determination (check one below):

    Use is Not Compatible

  X   Use is Compatible with Following Stipulations

Stipulations Necessary to Ensure Compatibility: Permits prior to construction will be obtained from local, state, and federal regulatory agencies to reduce the possibility of negatively impacting wetlands, cultural resources, or protected species. Law enforcement patrol of public use areas will continue to minimize violations of refuge regulations. Refuge roads will be closed to the public during extremely wet periods, such as flooding, to prevent road damage and for visitor safety. Public use for wildlife observation and photography will be monitored to document any negative impacts. If any negative impacts become noticeable, corrective action will be taken to reduce or eliminate the effects on wildlife.

Justification: Wildlife observation and photography are important and preferred public uses on Grand Cote Refuge and the National Wildlife Refuge System. The 1997 National Wildlife Refuge System Improvement Act identified wildlife observation and photography as a priority public recreational use to be facilitated on refuges. It is through permitted, compatible public uses such as this, that the public becomes aware of and provides support for national wildlife refuges.

Mandatory 15-year Re-evaluation Date: 11/17/2021

Description of Use: *Environmental Education and Interpretation*

Environmental education and interpretation are those activities which seek to increase the public's knowledge and understanding of wildlife, national wildlife refuges, ecology, and land management, as well as contribute to the conservation of natural resources. Interpretation and environmental education programs will be developed for the refuge. Environmental education/interpretation activities have been largely nonexistent in prior years. Efforts to develop this program are planned and will usually be associated with structured activities conducted by refuge staff or trained volunteers. Refuge staff will develop and provide curriculum and support materials to area teachers for use both on and off the refuge. Informational kiosks and interpretive panels will be developed at key refuge entrance points, and at the new boardwalk and wildlife observation platform.

Availability of Resources: Additional fiscal resources are needed to conduct these uses. Current staffing is extremely limited with no public use staff. The management of a volunteer program will be essential to successfully implement environmental education and interpretation programs. The addition of a permanent park ranger (interpretive)/public use specialist for the Complex, as identified in the Lake Ophelia Refuge Comprehensive Conservation Plan, will assist in providing environmental education and interpretation programs. Facilities, as well as vehicle access roads, boardwalks, signs, parking and trailhead development, kiosks, exhibit area at Headquarters' Office, and environmental education materials, also are needed to provide environmental education and interpretation activities.

Anticipated Impacts of the Use: Construction of boardwalks, kiosks, and observation platforms will alter small portions of the natural environment on the refuge. Proper planning and placement of facilities will ensure that wetlands, threatened or endangered species, or species of special concern are not negatively impacted. Proper permits through the parish, state, and federal regulatory agencies will be obtained prior to construction to ensure resource protection. The use of on-site, hands-on, action-oriented activities to accomplish environmental education and interpretive tours may impose a low-level impact on the sites used for these activities. These low-level impacts may include trampling of vegetation and temporary disturbance to wildlife species in the immediate area. Educational activities held off-refuge will not create any biological impacts on the resource.

Public Review and Comment: This compatibility determination was part of the Draft Comprehensive Conservation Plan and Environmental Assessment for Grand Cote National Wildlife Refuge, which was announced in the Federal Register and made available for public comment from June 16 – July 31, 2006 (71 FR 34955). Methods used to solicit public review and comment included posted notices at the refuge headquarters and other locations; copies of the draft comprehensive conservation plan and environmental assessment distributed to adjacent landowners, the public, and local, state, and federal agencies; public meetings; news releases to area newspapers; and local radio announcements. The availability of the draft plan/environmental assessment, the comment period, and public meeting location were announced in the Alexandria Daily Town Talk on June 25, 2006, and in the Avoyelles Journal on July 2, 2006.

Determination (check one below):

Use is Not Compatible

_X_ Use is Compatible with Following Stipulations

Stipulations Necessary to Ensure Compatibility: Zoning of visitor activities by time and space, clustering public use facilities, proper monitoring, educating visitors, and enforcement will ensure compatibility with the purposes of the refuge and mission of the National Wildlife Refuge System. Through periodic evaluation of trails and visitor contact points, the visitor services program will assess resource impacts. If future human impacts are determined through evaluation to be detrimental to important natural resources, actions will be taken to reduce or eliminate those impacts. Major portions of the refuge will remain undeveloped, without public interpretive facilities.

Justification: Environmental education and Interpretation are identified in the 1997 National Wildlife Refuge System Improvement Act as two of the six priority public uses made available on national wildlife refuges. Educating and informing the public through structured environmental education courses, interpretive materials, and guided tours about migratory birds, endangered species, wildlife management, and ecosystems will lead to improved support of the Service's mission to protect our natural resources.

Mandatory 15-year Re-evaluation Date: _11/17/2021_

Description of Use: All-terrain Vehicle Use

Recreational hunting is proposed on Grand Cote Refuge. A large portion of the refuge is inaccessible to conventional vehicles due to the lack of conventional roads. In order to disperse hunters and access remote areas for hunting, refuge users will need to utilize all-terrain vehicles throughout the area. There is an extensive system of old farm roads and levees that will be used as trails for these vehicles.

Considering the topography of the area, the need for limited use of all-terrain vehicles by certain refuge users is apparent. It would be impossible to develop an effective public use program that provides optimum consumptive use opportunities without providing for all-terrain vehicle use.

Service policy pertaining to all-terrain vehicle use requires such use be in conjunction with wildlife-dependent activities only, and be confined to designated areas or trails identified for such use; all off-road use is restricted to foot travel only. Approximately 5 miles of all-terrain trails will be available seasonally for hunting access. All-terrain vehicle trails are shown on refuge brochure maps and designated for public use by signs. Some modifications to this initial trail system will be necessary from time-to-time as refuge public use patterns change and/or other public use development occurs.

Availability of Resources: Enforcement of refuge regulations to protect trust resources and provide for a quality recreational opportunity will occur via regular patrols by refuge law enforcement officers. The headquarters for the Lake Ophelia Refuge Complex is located on Grand Cote Refuge, so these patrols will be performed more frequently than on other more remote refuges in the Complex. Currently, the Complex has one full-time officer and three collateral duty officers. Additionally, personnel from the Louisiana Department of Wildlife and Fisheries will patrol the refuge and assist officers when needed.

The hunt program at the refuge will cost approximately $25,000 annually, which includes costs to create and print the hunt brochure, provide law enforcement, and create and maintain parking areas and all-terrain vehicle trails. Participation in the hunt program is estimated to be between 500 and 1,000 visitors annually. The refuge is enrolled in the Recreational Fee Program and charges $15 for required hunt permits. Eighty percent of these funds will come back to the refuge to assist with the operation and management cost of having a hunt program.

Anticipated Biological Impacts of the Use: All-terrain vehicle trails are located on former field roads and levees that existed when the refuge was established. These trails have crown to provide drainage from the trail surface and are maintained by bush hogging two to three times per year. All-terrain vehicle use causes trampling of the mowed vegetation, but rutting and associated soil erosion should be very minimal. Some minimal wildlife disturbance may occur adjacent to the trails, but should be restricted to primarily the fall and winter months. Any disturbance from all-terrain vehicles will be comparable to regular vehicles traveling refuge roads. All-terrain vehicles will be restricted to designated marked trails.

Public Review and Comment: This compatibility determination was part of the Draft Comprehensive Conservation Plan and Environmental Assessment for Grand Cote National Wildlife Refuge, which was announced in the Federal Register and made available for public comment from June 16 – July 31, 2006 (71 FR 34955). Methods used to solicit public review and comment included posted notices at the refuge headquarters and other locations; copies of the draft comprehensive conservation plan and environmental assessment distributed to adjacent landowners, the public, and local, state, and federal agencies; public meetings; news releases to area newspapers; and local radio announcements. The availability of the draft plan/environmental assessment, the comment period, and public meeting location were announced in the Alexandria Daily Town Talk on June 25, 2006, and in the Avoyelles Journal on July 2, 2006.

Determination (check one below):

    Use is Not Compatible

  __X__ Use is Compatible with Following Stipulations

Stipulations Necessary to Ensure Compatibility: All-terrain vehicle use is permitted in support of hunting activities where adequate access is not available by maintained vehicular roads. The following stipulations will help ensure the refuge hunting program is compatible with refuge purposes:

- All persons over 16 years of age must have a Grand Cote Refuge hunting permit in order to use an all-terrain vehicle on the refuge.
- Persons under 16 years of age are not allowed to operate an all-terrain vehicle on the refuge.
- Use is restricted to designated and maintained all-terrain vehicle trails.
- No off-trail use of all-terrain vehicles is permitted.
- All-terrain vehicle tires are restricted to those no larger than 25"X12" with a maximum lug height of 1" and a maximum allowable tire pressure of 7 psi, as indicated on the tire by the manufacturer.
- All-terrain vehicles will not exceed the following specifications: weight – 750 lbs., length – 85", and width – 48".
- All weapons transported on all-terrain vehicles must be fully unloaded.
- All-terrain vehicle use is permitted only during daylight hours.

Justification: Hunting is identified in the 1997 National Wildlife Refuge System Improvement Act as a priority wildlife-dependent recreational activity that should be promoted and expanded on refuges. Grand Cote National Wildlife Refuge has very limited vehicular access to most portions of the refuge. To facilitate hunting, a limited system of all-terrain vehicle trails is required to provide access to major portions of the refuge and to specific lakes. Without these trails, the public would not be able to access major portions of the refuge.

Mandatory 10-year Re-evaluation Date: _11/17/2016_

Description of Use: Cooperative Farming Program

Cooperative farming is utilized on the refuge to manage and maintain approximately 2,650 acres of waterfowl impoundment habitats that provide seasonally flooded crops and moist-soil units necessary to meet the refuge's waterfowl habitat objectives. The farming program is a critical component of the refuge's habitat management program. The refuge's cooperative farmers enter into annual cooperative farming agreements specifying what crops will be grown in specific fields for both the refuge's and cooperative farmer's share. The cooperative farmer receives 80 percent of planted acres, while the refuge receives 20 percent of the planted acres. The refuge's crop share is strategically located in areas that can be flooded in the winter to provide waterfowl foraging habitat in support of North American Waterfowl Management Plan objectives for the Mississippi Alluvial Valley. At the present time, the refuge does not have the staff or equipment necessary to manage and maintain the acreage needed to meet its waterfowl foraging objectives without the assistance of the cooperative farming program. Refuge cooperative farming operations will continue under carefully regulated conditions.

Availability of Resources: Based on a review of the refuge's budget allocated for this activity, there is adequate funding to ensure compatibility and to administer the use at its current level.

Anticipated Impacts of the Use: Cooperative farmers grow grain, sorghum, rice, wheat, soybeans, and millet on the refuge under an annually updated cooperative farming agreement. Refuge crop shares are left standing in the field to provide high-energy grain and forage primarily for wintering waterfowl. The cooperative farmers' harvested fields are also used extensively by woodcock, waterfowl, deer, and wild turkeys. The majority of all cooperative farming takes place in the refuge's core waterfowl sanctuary area. Cooperative farmers also provide the equipment and personnel to manage the refuge's moist-soil units as part of the cooperative farming agreement.

Cooperative farming results in some degree of soil erosion due to spring disking and planting operations. The impact of soil erosion on adjacent wetlands and water bodies is minimal because of maintained grass buffer strips around each field and the extensive use of flash board risers to retain and slowly release sediment-laden water. Cooperative farmers are allowed to use approved pesticides under a closely monitored pesticide use proposal system. Refuge-approved pesticides have low toxicity and fast biodegradation rates compared to other commonly used agricultural pesticides. Under approved label application rates and methods, approved pesticides should have minimal effect on the biological environment. However, the potential exists for misapplication or accidental spills of approved pesticides. During the past 10 years, there have been no known pesticide accidents or pesticide-related wildlife mortality reported on the refuge. Careful monitoring of cooperative farmer pesticide use should further reduce any potential impacts from pesticide use on the refuge.

Public Review and Comment: This compatibility determination was part of the Draft Comprehensive Conservation Plan and Environmental Assessment for Grand Cote National Wildlife Refuge, which was announced in the Federal Register and made available for public comment from June 16 – July 31, 2006 (71 FR 34955). Methods used to solicit public review and comment included posted notices at the refuge headquarters and other locations; copies of the draft comprehensive conservation plan and environmental assessment distributed to adjacent landowners, the public, and local, state, and federal agencies; public meetings; news releases to area newspapers; and local radio announcements. The availability of the draft plan/environmental assessment, the comment period, and public meeting location were announced in the Alexandria Daily Town Talk on June 25, 2006, and in the Avoyelles Journal on July 2, 2006.

Determination (check one below):

Use is Not Compatible

__X__ Use is Compatible with Following Stipulations

Stipulations Necessary to Ensure Compatibility: The cooperative farming program is regulated through annual cooperative farming agreements that specify the field crops to be grown, acceptable farming practices, and approved pesticide-use procedures. Special conditions contained in each cooperative farming agreement provide the following requirements: no fall disking allowed, vegetative filter strips are maintained around all fields and water bodies, crops must be harvested by November 15 and no drainage of seasonally flooded habitat is allowed until after March 1. Refuge crops will be planted in designated fields and not be manipulated in any way after maturity; only approved pesticides will be used when the level of pest occurrence is at the economic threshold level as indicated by crop scouting. Under these carefully controlled conditions, the cooperative farming program has been and is expected to continue to be compatible with the refuge's purposes.

Justification: The cooperative farming actions as set forth in the Cropland Management Plan for Grand Cote National Wildlife Refuge are in accordance with Service guidelines for the protection, management, and enhancement of habitats for wildlife populations on the refuge. Adherence to the Cropland Management Plan promotes the enhancement of habitats for migratory birds, threatened and endangered species, and resident wildlife.

Mandatory 10 year Re-evaluation Date: 11/17/2016

Description of Use: *Research Studies*

This activity will allow university students and professors, non-governmental researchers, and governmental scientists access to the refuge's natural environment to conduct both short- and long-term research projects. The outcome of this research will result in better knowledge of our natural resources and improved methods to manage, monitor, and protect refuge resources. The refuge will support Service and U.S. Geological Survey research of neotropical migratory birds, waterfowl, woodcock, bottomland hardwood restoration, fisheries, amphibians and reptiles, forest bats, and sandhill cranes. Efforts will be made to expand partnerships with Louisiana State University and other universities.

Availability of Resources: No additional fiscal resources are needed to conduct this use. Existing staff can administer permits and monitor use as part of routine management duties.

Anticipated Impacts of the Use: There should be no significant negative impacts from scientific research on the refuge. The knowledge gained from the research will provide information to improve management techniques and better meet the needs of trust resource species. Impacts, such as trampling vegetation and temporary disturbance to wildlife, will occur but should not be significant. A small number of individual plants or animals may be collected for further study. These collections will have an insignificant effect on refuge plant and animal populations.

Public Review and Comment: This compatibility determination was part of the Draft Comprehensive Conservation Plan and Environmental Assessment for Grand Cote National Wildlife Refuge, which was announced in the Federal Register and made available for public comment from June 16 – July 31, 2006 (71 FR 34955). Methods used to solicit public review and comment included posted notices at the refuge headquarters and other locations; copies of the draft comprehensive conservation plan and environmental assessment distributed to adjacent landowners, the public, and local, state, and federal agencies; public meetings; news releases to area newspapers; and local radio announcements. The availability of the draft plan/environmental assessment, the comment period, and public meeting location were announced in the Alexandria Daily Town Talk on June 25, 2006, and in the Avoyelles Journal on July 2, 2006.

Determination (check one below):

        Use is Not Compatible

   X   Use is Compatible with Following Stipulations

Stipulations Necessary to Ensure Compatibility: Each request for use of the refuge for research will be examined on its individual merit. Questions of who, what, when, where, and why will be asked to determine if requested research contributed to the refuge purposes and could best be conducted on the refuge without significantly affecting the resources. If so, the researcher will be issued a special use permit. Progress will be monitored and the researcher will be required to submit annual progress reports and copies of all publications derived from the research.

Justification: The benefits derived from sound research provide a better understanding of species and the environmental communities present on the refuge. These benefits far outweigh any short-term disturbance or loss of individual plants and animals that might occur.

Mandatory 10-year Re-evaluation Date: 11/17/2016

Approval of Compatibility Determinations

The signature of approval is for all compatibility determinations considered within the Comprehensive Conservation Plan for Grand Cote National Wildlife Refuge. If one of the descriptive uses is considered for compatibility outside of the Comprehensive Conservation Plan, the approval signature becomes part of that determination.

Refuge Manager: _____ 8-10-06
                        (Signature/Date)

Regional Compatibility
Coordinator: _____ 8-28-06
                        (Signature/Date)

Refuge Supervisor: _____ 11/16/06
                        (Signature/Date)

Regional Chief, National
Wildlife Refuge System,
Southeast Region: _____ (Acting) 11-17-06
                        (Signature/Date)

Appendix VI. Intra-Service Section 7 Biological Evaluation

Originating Person: Michael P. Chouinard
Telephone Number: 318-253-4238
E-Mail: mike_chouinard@fws.gov
Date: November 1, 2005

Project Name: Grand Cote National Wildlife Refuge Comprehensive Conservation Plan

I.   **Service Program:**
___ **Ecological Services**
___ **Federal Aid**
___ **Clean Vessel Act**
___ **Coastal Wetlands**
___ **Endangered Species Section 6**
___ **Partners for Fish and Wildlife**
___ **Sport Fish Restoration**
___ **Wildlife Restoration**
___ **Fisheries**
_X_ **Refuges/Wildlife**

II.   **State/Agency:** Louisiana/U.S. Fish and Wildlife Service

III.   **Station Name:** Grand Cote National Wildlife Refuge

IV.   **Description of Proposed Action (attach additional pages as needed):** Implementation of the Comprehensive Conservation Plan for Grand Cote National Wildlife Refuge by adopting Alternative 2 as the preferred alternative, which will provide guidance, management direction, and operation plans for the next 15 years.

V.   **Pertinent Species and Habitat:**

A.   **Include species/habitat occurrence map:** The refuge is outside the known breeding range of Louisiana black bear (USFWS Louisiana Black Bear Recovery Plan 1995). It is highly unlikely that Louisiana black bears will move through or breed on the refuge.

Bald eagles are occasionally seen during winter months on the refuge. No breeding activity has been reported.

Interior least tern colonies have been documented on the Red River, which is not adjacent to the refuge.

B.   Complete the following table.

SPECIES/CRITICAL HABITAT	STATUS[1]
Louisiana black bear	T
Bald eagle	T
Interior least tern	E

[1]STATUS: E=endangered, T=threatened, PE=proposed endangered, PT=proposed threatened, CH=critical habitat, PCH=proposed critical habitat, C=candidate species

VI.   Location (attach map):

A.   **Ecoregion Number and Name:** Lower Mississippi Valley No. 27

B.   **County and State:** Avoyelles, Louisiana

C.   **Section, township, and range (or latitude and longitude):** T2N, T3N, R6E

D.   **Distance (miles) and direction to nearest town:** Ten miles east of Marksville, Louisiana

E.   **Species/habitat occurrence:**

Louisiana black bear--no documentation of bears using the refuge.

Bald eagle--occasionally observed during winter. No active nests.

Interior least tern--has known nesting colonies on Red River; however, not near the vicinity of the refuge.

VII.   Determination of Effects:

A.   **Explanation of effects of the action on species and critical habitats in item V. B (attach additional pages as needed).**

SPECIES/ CRITICAL HABITAT	IMPACTS TO SPECIES/CRITICAL HABITAT
Louisiana black bear	No negative impacts foreseen, more protection
Bald eagle	No negative impacts foreseen, more protection
Interior least tern	No negative impacts foreseen, more protection

B. Explanation of actions to be implemented to reduce adverse effects.

SPECIES/ CRITICAL HABITAT	ACTIONS TO MITIGATE/MINIMIZE IMPACTS
Louisiana black bear	Participate in recovery efforts by supporting repatriation efforts on Lake Ophelia Refuge
Bald eagle	Maintain and expand potential roosting and feeding habitat
Interior least tern	Work with Corps of Engineers and private landowners to maintain sandbar habitat along the Red River

VIII. Effect Determination and Response Requested:

SPECIES/ CRITICAL HABITAT	DETERMINATION[1]			RESPONSE[1] REQUESTED
	NE	NA	AA	
Louisiana black bear		X		
Bald eagle		X		
Interior least tern	X			

[1]*DETERMINATION/RESPONSE REQUESTED:*

NE = no effect. This determination is appropriate when the proposed action will not directly, indirectly, or cumulatively impact, either positively or negatively, any listed, proposed, candidate species or designated/proposed critical habitat. Response Requested is optional but a "Concurrence" is recommended for a complete Administrative Record.

NA = not likely to adversely affect. This determination is appropriate when the proposed action is not likely to adversely impact any listed, proposed, candidate species or designated/proposed critical habitat or there may be beneficial effects to these resources. Response Requested is a "Concurrence."

AA = likely to adversely affect. This determination is appropriate when the proposed action is likely to adversely impact any listed, proposed, candidate species or designated/proposed critical habitat. Response Requested for listed species is "Formal Consultation". Response Requested for proposed or candidate species is "Conference."

Signature (originating station)   11/23/05
                                         Date

Title   Active Refuge Manager

IX. Reviewing Ecological Services Office Evaluation:

   A. Concurrence _____✓   Nonconcurrence _____

B. Formal consultation required _____

C. Conference required _____

D. Informal conference required _____

E. Remarks (attach additional pages as needed):

_____   1/12/06
Signature   Date

Assistant Field Supervisor   LFO
Title   Office

Appendix VII. Refuge Biota

BIRDS
List taken from Vermillion and Walther 2001:
Pied-billed Grebe
American White Pelican
Double-crested Cormorant
Anhinga*
Black-crowned Night-Heron*
Yellow-crowned Night-Heron*
Green Heron*
Tricolored Heron
Little Blue Heron*
Snowy Egret
Cattle Egret*
Great Egret
Great Blue Heron*
American Bittern+
White Ibis
Turkey Vulture
Black Vulture
Greater White-fronted Goose
Snow Goose
Ross' Goose^
Wood Duck*
Green-winged Teal
American Black Duck^
Mottled Duck^
Mallard
Northern Pintail
Blue-winged Teal
Northern Shoveler
Gadwall
American Wigeon
Ring-necked Duck
Lesser Scaup
Bufflehead
Hooded Merganser
Ruddy Duck
Osprey

BIRDS
Bald Eagle!
Swallow-tailed Kite+^
Mississippi Kite*
Northern Harrier+
Sharp-shinned Hawk
Cooper's Hawk
Red-shouldered Hawk
Broad-winged Hawk
Red-tailed Hawk
American Kestrel
Merlin
Wild Turkey
Northern Bobwhite
Sora
Purple Gallinule*
Common Moorhen*
Killdeer
Greater Yellowlegs
Least Sandpiper
Common Snipe
American Woodcock
Herring Gull
Forster's Tern
Rock Dove
Mourning Dove*
Common Ground-Dove+
Yellow-billed Cuckoo*+
Eastern Screech-Owl
Great Horned Owl
Barred Owl
Common Nighthawk
Chimney Swift*
Ruby-throated Hummingbird
Belted Kingfisher*
Northern Flicker+
Red-bellied Woodpecker*
Red-headed Woodpecker*+^
Yellow-bellied Sapsucker
Downy Woodpecker

BIRDS
Hairy Woodpecker
Pileated Woodpecker
Eastern Pheobe
Eastern Wood-Pewee
Vermilion Flycatcher
Eastern Kingbird*
Great Crested Flycatcher
Acadian Flycatcher
Loggerhead Shrike*+
White-eyed Vireo*
Yellow-throated Vireo
Red-eyed Vireo*
Warbling Vireo
Solitary Vireo
Blue Jay*
American Crow*
Fish Crow
Horned Lark
Tree Swallow
Purple Martin*
Northern Rough-winged Swallow*
Barn Swallow*
Tufted Titmouse*
Carolina Chickadee*
White-breasted Nuthatch
Brown Creeper
Bewick's Wren+
House Wren
Winter Wren
Sedge Wren+
Marsh Wren
Carolina Wren*
Golden-crowned Kinglet
Ruby-crowned Kinglet
Blue-gray Gnatcatcher
Eastern Bluebird*
Hermit Thrush
Wood Thrush+^
American Robin

BIRDS
Northern Mockingbird*
Brown Thrasher*
Gray Catbird
European Starling*
American Pipit
Sprague's Pipit^
Cedar Waxwing
Orange-crowned Warbler
Nashville Warbler
Yellow-rumped Warbler
Prothonotary Warbler*^
Northern Parula
Black-and-White Warbler
Pine Warbler
Kentucky Warbler^
Hooded Warbler
Wilson's Warbler
Swainson's Warbler+^
Common Yellowthroat
American Redstart
Yellow-breasted Chat
Summer Tanager
Eastern Towhee
Chipping Sparrow
Field Sparrow+
Vesper Sparrow
Savannah Sparrow
Grasshopper Sparrow+
Henslow's Sparrow+^
LeConte's Sparrow
Fox Sparrow
Song Sparrow
Lincoln's Sparrow
Swamp Sparrow
White-throated Sparrow
White-crowned Sparrow
Northern Cardinal*
Blue Grosbeak
Indigo Bunting*

BIRDS
Painted Bunting+
Dickcissel*+
Eastern Meadowlark*+
Red-winged Blackbird*
Rusty Blackbird
Brown-headed Cowbird*
Common Grackle*
Orchard Oriole*
Baltimore Oriole*
House Finch
American Goldfinch
House Sparrow*

* - Confirmed as breeder in study area during 1994-1996 Louisiana Breeding Bird Atlas project (Vermillion and Walther 2001)
+ - U. S. Fish and Wildlife Service, Migratory Nongame Birds of Management Concern, 1995 List
^ - National Audubon Society Watch List species
! - Federally-listed species

MAMMALS
Armadillo*
Bats:
1) Southeastern myotis
2) Eastern pipistrelle
3) Red
4) Seminole
5) Hoary
6) Northern yellow
7) Evening
8) Rafinesque's big-eared
Beaver*
Bobcat*
Coyote*
Feral hogs*
Gray fox*
Red fox*
Long-tailed weasel
Mink*
Mice:
1) House
2) Deer

MAMMALS
3) Harvest
Nutria*
Opposum*
River Otter*
Raccoon*
Rats:
1) Wood
2) Rice
3) Cotton
Shrews:
1) Short-tailed
2) Least
Squirrels:
1) Gray*
2) Fox*
Striped skunk*
Rabbits:
1) Swamp*
2) Eastern Cottontail*
White-tailed deer*
Woodland vole

AMPHIBIANS AND REPTILES
Snakes
Timber rattlesnake*
Garter snake
Racer*
Eastern ribbon snake*
Rat snake*
King snake
Mud snake*
Copperhead*
Cottonmouth*
Various water snakes*
Frogs
Bullfrog*
Bronze frog*
Pig frog*

AMPHIBIANS AND REPTILES
Eastern narrowmouth toad*
Gray treefrog*
Green frog
Green treefrog*
Northern cricket frog*
Southern leopard frog*
Squirrel treefrog*
Spring peeper*
Upland chorus frog*
Woodhouse's toad*
Turtles
Alligator snapping turtle*
Cooters*
Eastern box turtle
False map turtle
Mississippi map turtle
Musk turtle
Painted turtle
Slider*
Snapping turtle*
Spiny softshell
Stinkpot*
Sirens, Newts, Salamanders, Lizards, Skinks, & Crocodilians
Lesser siren*
Central newt*
Mole salamander*
Green anole*
Eastern fence lizard
Broad-headed skink
Five-lined skink*
Ground skink*
Alligator*
*Species known to occur on, near, or in similar habitats to Grand Cote NWR

MUSSELS
Fat pocketbook
Flat floater
Giant floater
Mapleleaf

MUSSELS
Paper pondshell
Papershell
Pink papershell
Pondmussel
Southern mapleleaf
Texas lilliput
Yellow sandshell

FISH
Bluegill
Longear sunfish
Orange spotted sunfish
Redear sunfish
Warmouth
Green sunfish
White crappie
Black crappie
Largemouth bass
Yellow bass
Freshwater drum
Black bullheads
Yellow bullheads
Channel catfish
Flathead catfish
Bigmouth buffalo
Smallouth buffalo
Spotted gar
Shortnose gar
Longnose gar
Alligator gar
Carp
Bowfin

VEGETATION
Trees - Dominant Vegetation
Black willow
Cherrybark willow
Cottonwood

VEGETATION
Bald cypress
Drummond red maple
Elms: winged, water, cedar
Green ash
Gum -red, tupelo
Hackberry
Oaks: overcup, Nuttall, Shumard, water, willow
Pecans -- sweet and bitter
Red maple
Red mulberry
Swamp Cottonwood
Sweetgum
Sycamore
Mid-story/Understory -Subdominant vegetation
Black berry
Black locust
Box elder
Button bush
Deciduous holly
Dew berry
French mulberry
Haws (cretagus)
Honey locust
Honey suckle
Hornbeam palmetto
Persimmon
Prickly ash
Smilax
Swamp dogwood
Swamp privet
Switchcane
Vines: rattan, muscadine, poison ivy and oak, Virginia creeper, pepper vine, cross vine and grape
Water hickory
Water locust
Wet Sites
Pickerel-weed
Water hyacinth
Pennywort
Duckweed

VEGETATION
Arrowhead
Smartweed
Water primrose
American lotus
Coontail
Floating heart
various sedges and grasses
Iris
Spider lily
Lizards tail
Marsh mallow
Cardinal flower

Appendix VIII. List of Preparers

Introduction

The Grand Cote National Wildlife Refuge comprehensive conservation planning process involved a wide variety of participants, including federal, state, and local governments; universities and other researchers; private non-profit groups; and local residents. The diversity and input of participants helped guide development of the plan and this environmental assessment. A core planning team led the process, a Biological and Habitat Review Team helped develop wildlife and habitat needs, a Visitor Services Team helped develop public use needs, and the public contributed to the process during the scoping period. Section A, Chapter III, describes the public's involvement in this planning process.

Core Planning Team Members

The Core Planning Team involved staff from the Central Louisiana National Wildlife Refuge Complex. This team was the primary decision-making team for the comprehensive conservation plan. Key tasks of the team involved defining and refining the vision; identifying, reviewing, and filtering issues; defining the goals; and outlining the alternatives. The team members included:

- Mike Chouinard, Jr., Project Leader, Central Louisiana NWR Complex
- Ben Mense, Deputy Project Leader (former), Central Louisiana NWR Complex
- Mindy Gautreaux, Deputy Project Leader (current), Central Louisiana NWR Complex
- Richard Crossett, Wildlife Biologist, Central Louisiana NWR Complex
- Tina Chouinard, Natural Resource Planner, Central Louisiana NWR Complex

Biological and Habitat Review Team

The Biological and Habitat Review Team consisted of Service staff and invited participants. The invited participants included local and regional experts, researchers, and individuals with intimate knowledge of and expertise in the biological resources of the refuge. Members of the review team included:

- Mike Chouinard, Project Leader — Fish and Wildlife Service
- Ben Mense, Deputy Project Leader — Fish and Wildlife Service
- Richard Crossett, Wildlife Biologist — Fish and Wildlife Service
- Tina Chouinard, Natural Resource Planner — Fish and Wildlife Service
- Richard Dupuy, Maintenance Worker — Fish and Wildlife Service
- James Baker, Refuge Manager — Fish and Wildlife Service
- Jimmy Anthony, Program Manager — Louisiana Department of Wildlife and Fisheries
- Robby Howard, District Biologist — Ducks Unlimited
- Randy Lanctot, Executive Director — Louisiana Wildlife Federation
- Pat Stinson, Wildlife Biologist, Forester — Fish and Wildlife Service
- Andy Dolan, Fish and Wildlife Biologist — Fish and Wildlife Service
- Charles Guillory, Soil Scientist — Natural Resources Conservation Service
- Steve Cruse, State WRP Coordinator — Natural Resources Conservation Service
- John Pitre, State Biologist — Natural Resources Conservation Service
- Buddy Dupuy, Forester — Louisiana Department of Wildlife and Fisheries

- Chuck Hunter, Regional Refuge Biologist   Fish and Wildlife Service
- Sammy King, Leader/Professor   U.S.G.S/Louisiana State
- Kerney Sonnier, District Biologist   Louisiana Department of Wildlife and Fisheries
- Kenny Ribbeck, Biologist   Louisiana Department of Wildlife and Fisheries
- Bob Strader, Supervisory Wildlife Biologist   Fish and Wildlife Service
- Bill Vermillion, Biologist   Fish and Wildlife Service
- Barry Wilson, Evaluation Coordinator   Ducks Unlimited – Gulf Coast Joint Venture

Visitor Service Review Team

The Visitor Service Review Team consisted of Fish and Wildlife Service staff from the Southeast Regional Office and the Washington Office. Members of the review team included:

- Garry Tucker   Visitor Services and Outreach, RO
- Steve Farrell   Visitor Services and Communication, WO
- Tom Prusa   Area IV Assistant Refuge Supervisor, RO
- Tina Chouinard   Natural Resource Planner, Central Louisiana NWR Complex

Appendix IX. Budget Requests

REFUGE OPERATING NEEDS AND SERVICE ASSET MAINTENANCE MANAGEMENT SYSTEM

Grand Cote NWR Operating and Maintenance Needs

Project Number	CCP Project Description Number	Project Description	Cost Estimate ($1000's)
FISH AND WILDLIFE POPULATIONS			
RONS 97007	2/3	Control Invasive Plant Pest in Lakes and Moist Soil Units	127
RONS 00032	9	Refuge Private Lands Conservation Initiative	151
HABITATS			
RONS 00005	3	Soil and Water Conservation Best Management Practices (Maintenance Worker Position)	128
RONS 00025	3/4/5	Perform Moist Soil Management and Maintain Water Management Infrastructure	120
RONS 00030	3/4/5	Plan and Implement Wetland Restoration within Refuge Complex (Assistant Refuge Manager)	151
RONS 00008	3/4	Water Management System Maintenance	124
SAMMS 98123259	3/4/5	Improve water delivery to flooded habitats.	100
SAMMS 2005204509	3/4	Replace Water Control Structures 66, 67,68	26
VISITOR SERVICES			
RONS 97003	12/13	Provide Visitor Services and Education Programs	151
RONS 00023	12/13	Visitor Center Operations	225
RONS 00024	12/13	Visitor Center Operations	34
SAMMS 2005206150	14	Rehabilitate Bascum Road	188
SAMMS 123134	13	Construct parking areas equipped with directional	48
SAMMS 123153	12/13	Construct Wildlife observation area facilities.	141
SAMMS 123261	12/13	Construct Environmental education/interpretive program	270

Project Number	CCP Project Description Number	Project Description	Cost Estimate ($1000's)
SAMMS 2005219911	12/13	Construct Wildlife observation facilities	70
SAMMS 4134730	14	Rehabilitate 0.5-mile deteriorated Pumpout road	374
SAMMS 2005203947	14	Rehabilitate Pumpout Road	50
SAMMS 102050	14	Rehabilitate 3 miles of dirt road	150
SAMMS 102048	14	Rehabilitate 1.5 miles of the Bascum Road	500
SAMMS 102049	14	Rehabilitate 1 mile of Lachney road and two parking areas	125
SAMMS 2005203318	14	Remove Choctaw Bayou Bridge	26
SAMMS 2119135	16	Replace 11 pipe gates on Grand Cote Refuge	28
REFUGE ADMINISTRATION			
SAMMS 98110073	17	Construct new maintenance and storage buildings	1406
SAMMS 2119110	18	Replace HEQ 2000 John Deere 6410 Tractor	73
SAMMS 2119063	18	Replace SEQ 2002 Chevrolet CK15753 Truck	31
SAMMS 2119062	18	Replace SEQ 2002 GMC CK15753 Chevrolet truck	31
SAMMS 2119111	18	Replace HEQ 2002 John Deere 7610 Tractor	96

Appendix X. Finding of No Significant Impact

Introduction
The U.S. Fish and Wildlife Service proposes to protect and manage certain fish and wildlife resources in Avoyelles Parish, Louisiana, through the Grand Cote National Wildlife Refuge. An Environmental Assessment has been prepared to inform the public of the possible environmental consequences of implementing the Comprehensive Conservation Plan for Grand Cote National Wildlife Refuge. A description of the alternatives, the rationale for selecting the preferred alternative, the environmental effects of the preferred alternative, the potential adverse effects of the action, and a declaration concerning the factors determining the significance of effects, in compliance with the National Environmental Policy Act of 1969, are outlined below. The supporting information can be found in the Environmental Assessment, which was Section B of the Draft Comprehensive Conservation Plan for Grand Cote National Wildlife Refuge.

Alternatives
In developing the Comprehensive Conservation Plan for Grand Cote National Wildlife Refuge, the Fish and Wildlife Service evaluated three alternatives: Alternative 1 (no action); Alternative 2 (active management); and Alternative 3 (restoration of endemic ecosystem).

The Service adopted Alternative 2, the "Preferred Alternative," as the comprehensive conservation plan for guiding the direction of the refuge for the next 15 years. The overriding concern reflected in this plan is that wildlife conservation assumes first priority in refuge management and wildlife-dependent recreational uses are allowed if they are compatible with wildlife conservation. Wildlife-dependent recreation uses (e.g., hunting, fishing, wildlife observation, wildlife photography, and environmental education and interpretation) will be emphasized and encouraged.

Alternative 1 represents no change from current management of the refuge. Under this alternative, 6,075 acres of refuge lands would be protected, maintained, restored, and enhanced for resident wildlife, waterfowl, and threatened and endangered species. Refuge management programs would continue to be developed and implemented with little baseline biological information. All management actions would be directed toward achieving the refuge's primary purposes (e.g., conserving wintering habitat for mallards, pintails, blue-winged teal, and wood duck; providing production habitat for wood ducks; and helping to meet the habitat conservation goals of the North American Waterfowl Management Plan), while contributing to other national, regional, and state goals. Cooperative farming would continue to be used to manage and maintain approximately 2,400 acres of cropland and moist-soil habitats. The current level of wildlife-dependent recreation activities (e.g., hunting, fishing, wildlife observation, wildlife photography, and environmental education and interpretation) would be maintained.

The preferred alternative, Alternative 2, is considered to be the most effective management action for meeting the purposes of the refuge by adding more staff, equipment, and facilities in order to manage and restore the refuge's wetland and moist-soil habitats and hydrology in support of migratory and resident waterfowl and other wildlife, especially white-tailed deer and woodcock. The preferred alternative seeks to conduct extensive wildlife population monitoring/surveying in order to assess population status, trends, wildlife habitat associations, and population responses to habitat management. Active habitat management will be implemented through water level manipulations, moist-soil and cropland management, minimal reforestation, and forest management designed to provide a diverse complex of habitats that meets the foraging, resting, and breeding requirements for a variety of species. Cooperative farming will be used to manage and maintain approximately 1,940 acres of existing refuge cropland and moist-soil habitats. Under this alternative, the refuge will continue to seek acquisition of inholdings from all willing sellers within the present acquisition boundary. The refuge will seek to protect an additional 2,500 – 3,000 acres from willing sellers in the Chatlain Lake acquisition area to help better meet waterfowl objectives. The six priority wildlife-dependent public uses will continue to be supported and in some cases they will be expanded throughout the refuge under the preferred alternative. This alternative will also strengthen the close working relationship in existence between the Service, the local community, conservation organizations, the Louisiana Department of Wildlife and Fisheries, and other state and federal agencies.

The primary focus under Alternative 3 would be to maximize bottomland hardwood forest restoration in support of the endemic habitat for this area. Under this alternative, 6,075 acres of refuge lands would be protected, maintained, restored, and enhanced for resident wildlife, waterfowl, neotropical migratory birds, and threatened and endangered species. Some wildlife and plant censuses and inventory activities would be initiated to obtain the biological information needed to implement management programs, especially for forest-dependent species. Most management actions would be directed toward creating and managing the bottomland hardwood forest habitat (for neotropical migratory birds and other forest-dependent wildlife) while supporting the refuge's primary purposes. Cooperative farming would be eliminated. Agricultural acreage would be reduced to 500 acres; all farming would be conducted by refuge staff. The refuge would maintain 400 acres of moist-soil habitat. Under this alternative, the refuge would continue to seek acquisition of all willing-seller properties within the present refuge boundary; however, the Service would eliminate the Chatlain Lake area from the current acquisition boundary. Quality wildlife-dependent recreation (e.g., hunting, fishing, wildlife observation, wildlife photography, and environmental education and interpretation) opportunities would be provided.

Selection Rationale
Alternative 2 is selected for implementation because it directs the development of programs to best achieve the refuge purpose and goals; emphasizes management and restoration of the refuge's wetland and moist-soil habitats and hydrology in support of migratory and resident waterfowl and other wildlife, especially white-tailed deer, wood duck, and woodcock; collects habitat and wildlife data; and ensures long-term achievement of refuge and Service objectives. At the same time, these management actions provide balanced levels of compatible public use opportunities consistent with existing laws, Service policies, and sound biological principles. It provides the best mix of program elements to achieve desired long-term conditions.

Under this alternative, all lands under the management and direction of the refuge will be protected, maintained, and enhanced and those lands within the approved acquisition boundary will be prioritized for acquisition to best achieve national, regional, ecosystem, and refuge-specific goals and objectives within anticipated funding and staffing levels. In addition, the action positively addresses significant issues and concerns expressed by the public.

Environmental Effects
Implementation of the Service's management action is expected to result in environmental, social, and economic effects as outlined in the comprehensive conservation plan. Habitat management, fish and wildlife population management, resource protection, and visitor service management activities on Grand Cote National Wildlife Refuge will result in increased migratory bird utilization and production; enhanced native resident wildlife populations; and enhanced opportunities for wildlife-dependent recreation and environmental education. These effects are detailed as follows:

1. Duck and shorebird use of the refuge will improve significantly as intensive water management upgrades and efforts will provide dependable flooded habitats to match the migration chronologies of these species. Woodcock population numbers and habitat use will be monitored and managed and woodcock use of the refuge will be expected to increase.

2. Migratory bird production will increase by enhancing habitat and food availability for wintering waterfowl, habitat management for resident species, and through hydrological restoration and management.

3. Refuge land acquisition and protection will greatly improve the refuge's access, ability to meet step-down objectives for waterfowl and other wildlife species, and provide more opportunities for public use.

4. The refuge's habitat mix of cropland, early successional reforestation areas, bottomland hardwood forest, and upland forest, as well as habitat management, will improve food and cover for resident wildlife species and enhance wetland communities within the refuge.

5. Habitat restoration and management, along with a focus on accessibility and facility developments, will result in improved wildlife-dependent recreational opportunities. While public use will result in some minimal, short-term adverse effects on wildlife and user conflicts may occur at certain times of the year, these effects are minimized by site design, time zoning, and implementing refuge regulations. Anticipated long-term impacts to wildlife and wildlife habitats of implementing the management action are positive. In the long run, wildlife habitat and increased opportunities for wildlife-dependent recreation opportunities could result in an increase in economic benefits to the local community.

6. Implementing the comprehensive conservation plan is not expected to have any significant adverse effects on wetlands and floodplains, pursuant to Executive Orders 11990 and 11988, as actions will not result in development of buildings and/or structures within floodplain areas, nor will they result in irrevocable, long-term adverse impacts. In fact, a major thrust of the management action is to implement bottomland hardwood forest and open wetland restoration within the wildlife communities of the refuge that has been severely impacted by actions of previous landowners. Implementing the management action will result in substantial enhancement of forest and open wetland communities and net increases to the Nation's bottomland hardwood forest and open wetland acreage and quality.

Potential Adverse Effects and Mitigation Measures

Wildlife Disturbance
Disturbance to wildlife at some level is an unavoidable consequence of any public use program, regardless of the activity involved. Obviously, some activities innately have the potential to be more disturbing than others. The management actions to be implemented have been carefully planned to avoid unacceptable levels of impact.

As currently proposed, the known and anticipated levels of disturbance of the management action are considered minimal and well within the tolerance level of known wildlife species and populations present in the area. Implementation of the public use program will take place through carefully controlled time and space zoning, establishment of protection zones around key sites, closures of all-terrain vehicle trails, and routing of roads and trails to avoid direct contact with sensitive areas, such as nesting bird habitat. All hunting activities (e.g., season lengths, bag limits, and number of hunters) will be conducted within the constraints of sound biological principles and refuge-specific regulations established to restrict illegal or non-conforming activities. Monitoring activities through wildlife inventories and assessments of public use levels and activities will be utilized, and public use programs will be adjusted as needed to limit disturbance.

User Group Conflicts
As public use levels expand across time, some conflicts between user groups may occur. Programs will be adjusted, as needed, to eliminate or minimize these problems and provide quality wildlife-dependent recreational opportunities. Experience has proven that time and space zonings, such as establishment of separate use areas, use periods, and restricting numbers of users, are effective tools in eliminating conflicts between user groups.

Effects on Adjacent Landowners
Implementation of the management action will not impact adjacent or in-holding landowners. Essential access to private property will be allowed through issuance of special use permits. Future land acquisition will occur on a willing-seller basis only, at fair market values within the approved acquisition boundary. Lands are acquired through a combination of fee title purchases and/or donations and less-than-fee title interests (e.g., conservation easements and cooperative agreements) from willing sellers. Funds for the acquisition of lands within the approved acquisition boundary will likely come from the Land and Water Conservation Fund or the Migratory Bird Conservation Act. The management action contains neither provisions nor proposals to pursue off-refuge stream bank riparian zone protection measures (e.g., fencing) other than on a volunteer/partnership basis.

Land Ownership and Site Development
Proposed acquisition efforts by the Service will result in changes in land and recreational use patterns, since all uses on national wildlife refuges must meet compatibility standards. Land ownership by the Service also precludes any future economic development by the private sector. Potential development of access roads, dikes, control structures, and visitor parking areas could lead to minor short-term negative impacts on plants, soil, and some wildlife species. When site development activities are proposed, each activity will be given the appropriate National Environmental Policy Act consideration during pre-construction planning. At that time, any required mitigation activities will be incorporated into the specific project to reduce the level of impacts to the human environment and to protect fish and wildlife and their habitats.

As indicated earlier, one of the direct effects of site development is increased public use; this increased use may lead to littering, noise, and vehicle traffic. While funding and personnel resources will be allocated to minimize these effects, such allocations make these resources unavailable for other programs.

The management action is not expected to have significant adverse effects on wetlands and floodplains, pursuant to Executive Orders 11990 and 11988.

Coordination
The management action has been thoroughly coordinated with all interested and/or affected parties. Parties contacted include:

All affected landowners
Congressional representatives
Governor of Louisiana
Louisiana Department of Wildlife and Fisheries
Louisiana State Historic Preservation Officer

Louisiana Department of Natural Resources, Coastal Management Division
Kisatchie-Delta Regional Planning and Economic Development District
Local community officials
Interested citizens
Conservation organizations

Findings
It is my determination that the management action does not constitute a major federal action significantly affecting the quality of the human environment under the meaning of Section 102(2)(c) of the National Environmental Policy Act of 1969 (as amended). As such, an environmental impact statement is not required. This determination is based on the following factors (40 C.F.R. 1508.27), as addressed in the Environmental Assessment for Grand Cote National Wildlife Refuge:

1. Both beneficial and adverse effects have been considered and this action will not have a significant effect on the human environment. (Environmental Assessment, pages 105-118).

2. The actions will not have a significant effect on public health and safety. (Environmental Assessment, pages 105-118).

3. The project will not significantly affect any unique characteristics of the geographic area such as proximity to historical or cultural resources, wild and scenic rivers, or ecologically critical areas. (Environmental Assessment, pages 105-118).

4. The effects on the quality of the human environment are not likely to be highly controversial. (Environmental Assessment, pages 105-118).

5. The actions do not involve highly uncertain, unique, or unknown environmental risks to the human environment. (Environmental Assessment, pages 105-118).

6. The actions will not establish a precedent for future actions with significant effects nor do they represent a decision in principle about a future consideration. (Environmental Assessment, pages 105-118).

7. There will be no cumulatively significant impacts on the environment. Cumulative impacts have been analyzed with consideration of other similar activities on adjacent lands, in past action, and in foreseeable future actions. (Environmental Assessment, pages 105-118).

8. The actions will not significantly affect any site listed in, or eligible for listing in, the National Register of Historic Places, nor will they cause loss or destruction of significant scientific, cultural, or historic resources. (Environmental Assessment, pages 105-118).

9. The actions are not likely to adversely affect threatened or endangered species, or their habitats. (Environmental Assessment, pages 105-118).

10. The actions will not lead to a violation of federal, state, or local laws imposed for the protection of the environment. (Environmental Assessment, pages 105-118).

Supporting References
Fish and Wildlife Service. 2006. Draft Comprehensive Conservation Plan and Environmental Assessment for Grand Cote National Wildlife Refuge, Avoyelles Parish, Louisiana. U.S. Department of the Interior, Fish and Wildlife Service, Southeast Region.

Document Availability
The Environmental Assessment was Section B of the Draft Comprehensive Conservation Plan for Grand Cote National Wildlife Refuge and was made available in May 2006. Additional copies are available by writing: Grand Cote National Wildlife Refuge, 401 Island Road, Marksville, Louisiana 71341.

Noreen E Walsh   9/25/06

Acting Sam D. Hamilton   Date
Regional Director